Growing Old with the Welfare State

ALSO AVAILABLE FROM BLOOMSBURY

State and Society: A Social and Political History of Britain since 1870 (5th Edition), Martin Pugh (2017)

The British Welfare Revolution, 1906-14, John Cooper (2017)

1938: Modern Britain, Michael John Law (2017)

When the Girls Come Out to Play, Katharine Milcoy (2017)

Leisure, Voluntary Action and Social Change in Britain, 1880-1939, Robert Snape (2018)

The Women's Liberation Movement and the Politics of Class in Britain, George Stevenson (2019)

Growing Old with the Welfare State

Eight British Lives

EDITED BY
NICK HUBBLE, JENNIE TAYLOR AND PHILIP TEW

BLOOMSBURY ACADEMIC
LONDON • NEW YORK • OXFORD • NEW DELHI • SYDNEY

BLOOMSBURY ACADEMIC
Bloomsbury Publishing Plc
50 Bedford Square, London, WC1B 3DP, UK
1385 Broadway, New York, NY 10018, USA

BLOOMSBURY, BLOOMSBURY ACADEMIC and the Diana logo are
trademarks of Bloomsbury Publishing Plc

First published in Great Britain 2019

Cover design: Adriana Brioso
Cover image: A group of elderly people relax in deckchairs on the beach at Brighton
Beach, West Sussex, 1966. (© Tony Ray-Jones/SSPL/Getty Images)

A catalogue record for this book is available from the British Library.

A catalog record for this book is available from the Library of Congress.

ISBN:	HB:	978-1-3500-3310-8
	PB:	978-1-3500-3309-2
	ePDF:	978-1-3500-3312-2
	eBook:	978-1-3500-3311-5

Typeset by Integra Software Services Pvt. Ltd.
Printed and bound in Great Britain

To find out more about our authors and books visit www.bloomsbury.com
and sign up for our newsletters.

To our respective partners

Contents

Acknowledgements

The editors of *Growing Old with the Welfare State* wish to first acknowledge the financial and other support provided by the New Dynamics of Ageing (NDA) Programme involved in funding the original research on which this volume draws, the Fiction and Cultural Mediation of Ageing Project (FCMAP), overseen by the Economic and Social Research Council on behalf of this unique cross-research council initiative. Thanks too to those at the Research Support and Development Office (RSDO) at Brunel and at the think tank Demos who helped shape the initial application and additionally to Louise Bazalgette and John Holden at Demos for various insights they offered during the research process. During the course of the original research project, we were ably assisted by Natalia Clarke and subsequently Denise Odell, the FCMAP administrators. This book directly results from the follow-on project to FCMAP, 'New Narratives of Everyday Ageing in Contemporary Britain', funded by the Economic and Social Research Council (ESRC).

We would also like to thank all those who took part as respondents in the two strands of FCMAP, both under the aegis of Mass Observation (MO) and the London and Banstead districts of the University of the Third Age (U3A). In particular, we are deeply grateful for the participation and enthusiasm of the contributors included in this volume, without whom the book would simply not exist. We would further like to acknowledge the immense efforts in support of our research made by Jennifer Anning and Keith Richards of the U3A. With regard to MO staff, we would like to thank Dorothy Sheridan for initial discussions of the FCMAP project and help in framing the MO directive sent out late in 2009 and Jessica Scantlebury for ongoing liaison over the directive and her assistance with MO archival material alongside Fiona Courage, Rose Lock, Joe Williams and everyone else working in Special Collections formerly held at the University of Sussex Library and now across the road in the Keep, Falmer. We thank the Trustees of the Mass-Observation Archive for permission to quote MO material. We are also grateful to Gordon Wise, Richard Pike and Niall Harmon at Curtis Brown for their help in organizing the publication of this book with Bloomsbury and to Beatriz Lopez, Dan Hutchins and their colleagues at Bloomsbury.

Also worthy of mention is Dr Jago Morrison of Brunel University who as a participating member of the FCMAP research team helped both develop and shape the original project, after which he continued to offer suggestions throughout the process. Responding to his interventions helped refine our methodological and analytical approaches.

Introduction

Growing Old with the Welfare State presents extracts from the stories of eight British people born between 1921 and 1943, who record and celebrate on a personal level various radical and important shifts in both their own lives and British cultural life over the last century. As described below and in more detail in the appendix to this book, these stories come from a research project called 'Fiction and the Cultural Mediation of Ageing' (FCMAP) that was carried out by the Brunel Centre for Contemporary Writing (BCCW) at Brunel University London as part of the UK-wide New Dynamics of Ageing (NDA) research programme, coordinated by Professor Alan Walker (Sheffield University) for the Economic and Social Research Council (ESRC). This Brunel research project was carried out in collaboration with the Mass Observation (MO) Project and University of the Third Age (U3A) groups from the London and Banstead districts. Six of our writers are from MO and two of them are from the U3A.

In the 1960s, youth became a cultural fixation and permeated a whole plethora of fields and activities, displacing the traditional and the staid from view. However, as the baby boomers aged and the demographic balance has shifted dramatically, ageing itself is perhaps at last becoming trendy. One only has to consider the popularity of Diana Athill or Penelope Lively's celebration of old age in the Guardian on the occasion of her eightieth birthday in 2013 to see how the zeitgeist has shifted so rapidly over the past decade. People now admire and, even, envy those in the retired age ranges for their continued enthusiasm, their varied lifestyles and their apparent, outward financial security. Our intention for Growing Old with the Welfare State was to contribute to this ongoing cultural phenomenon by bringing together a selection of ordinary people reflecting on their lives over a period of sixty plus years by discussing how they live now and how they got to this point in time – the past the prologue to the present.

This intention is still reflected in the book in front of you, but it has become subtly altered following the completion of the original FCMAP and further time to reflect properly on its results and conclusions. As noted in the book that two of us wrote following that project, *Ageing, Narrative and Identity*, 'our public and social concept of "successful ageing" has to be revised' (Hubble and Tew 2013: 199). This is because such notions as 'successful' or 'active' ageing suggest a subtle orthodoxy that there is such a thing as 'unsuccessful' or 'inactive' ageing. The implicit message is that those unable, perhaps for reasons of health or lack of resources, to participate in the celebratory ageing zeitgeist of good health and outward orientation are somehow to blame for their own lack of success over the life course. In particular, we argued that the conventional understanding of the 'third' and 'fourth' ages as respectively a post-retirement age of personal fulfilment and a final era of 'dependence, decrepitude and death' (Laslett 1996: 4) needed to be rethought. While there has undoubtedly been a major social revolution by which third-agers in their sixties, seventies and eighties are now living completely different lifestyles to those of the mid-twentieth century, the challenge of this paradigmatic change for society as a whole is not just to stop considering people in these age ranges as old but

> to ensure that the consequent expansion of third age identification is not based on subjects defining themselves against a fourth age of decline and death. As we have shown, there is now the possibility of positively defining a new understanding of the fourth age in which it is possible to accept that one has become old and perhaps infirm, but still partaking of and contributing to life and society. Such a successful fourth age is a product of reflective narrative. (Hubble and Tew 2013: 200)

By reflective narrative, we mean the kind of life writing promoted by MO and made familiar to the general reading public through the publication of individual diaries such as *Nella Last's War* (1981) – memorably dramatized for television as *Housewife, 49* (2006) by the late Victoria Wood who also won a BAFTA for her performance in the main role – or the three collections edited by Simon Garfield: *Our Hidden Lives* (2004), *We Are at War* (2005) and *Private Battles* (2006). As James Hinton (2010) argues, MO writing has a unique specificity: 'Mass-Observation offered a discipline and a context which transcended the purely private, meeting a need to frame individual quests in relation to larger public purposes' (6). He adds that the wartime diaries 'take us as close as a historian can hope to get to observe selfhood under construction' (7). In a similar manner, we found the writing of both our MO and U3A co-researchers (for that is how the contribution of our project participants should really be perceived) capable of taking us as close as we could hope to get to observing a new type of fourth-age selfhood under construction. Following project participant narratives, either in the reflective reading diaries and autobiographies of U3A members or across the extensive directive responses dating back to 1981 of MO panel members (see Appendix for details of how this material was collected), not only could we see the wave of social change enabled by post-war stability and prosperity and the overwhelming sense of liberation felt at the moment of retirement under these circumstances as new horizons opened on what for many turned out to be the happiest and most fulfilling times of their lives but also, after fifteen to twenty-five years of liberated life, we saw that the eventual recognition, 'and now I *am* old' (qtd. Hubble and Tew 2013: 77), was not generally a harbinger of doom but an opportunity to move on to something different, from sailing to WEA classes perhaps, and to take pride in the ability to look back and learn from one's life. The point is that ageing is a continual process that cannot be reduced to the essence of one particular phase of post-retirement lifestyle considered in contrast against a supposed final phase of decline and death. In fact, the experience of ageing changes as continually in later years as it does in earlier or middle years: ageing is a lifelong process! As Anne Karpf (2014) argues, ageing across the entire lifespan is about enrichment and growth, and the later years in particular 'can be actively enriching, a time of immense growth. Perhaps that's why it's called "growing old"' (3). It is precisely in this spirit and understanding that the title of *Growing Old with the Welfare State* was chosen for this volume. Hopefully, the rich and complex life stories collected here demonstrate that continual process of growth across the lifespan, offering a sociocultural evolutionary sense of ageing.

Turning to the other component of this book's title, the 'Welfare State', it is worth noting that although the term is now embedded in everyday language, both the history of its usage and the extent of what it defines are varied and often context dependent. In his *The Five Giants: A Biography of the Welfare State*, originally published in 1995, Nicholas Timmins notes that the term extends from the narrow American definition of welfare as payments to the poor to 'virtually the whole of the economic and social history of Britain from 1945' and notes that his own coverage is restricted to 'the mainstream services of health, education, social security, housing, social services, and, in lesser detail, employment policy' (7). In our usage of the term, we are following Timmins's own practice. Although it is perfectly valid to think of a more-encompassing sense of the Welfare State – including social-democratic and collective values as manifested through nationalized industries and corporate approaches to business – as typifying the political and social culture of post-war Britain from 1945 to 1975, the advantage of Timmins's approach is that it allows us to focus on those welfare mechanisms which have persisted beyond the Thatcherite rejection of the collective and corporate aspects of the post-war British state and continued to support the lives of retired generations – including our featured writers – into the twenty-first century. Nonetheless, it should be noted that the dissonance between all three of these concepts of the 'Welfare State' is also an enduring aspect of British life and can be detected within some of the narratives collected in this volume.

Less controversial than the definition of the Welfare State perhaps is the widespread perception that the pattern of the human life course in Britain changed irrevocably over the second half of the last century as a direct result of the introduction of universal health, education and social security provisions, as well as a steady increase of the possibility of entering higher education. The combined effect of the Welfare State and medical advances mean that more people now live longer, happier and healthier lives than ever before in recorded human history. As a consequence of these changes, the experience of ageing has been completely transformed. While forty years ago retirement was envisioned as pottering about in the garden and taking to an armchair, it is now just another different active phase of life. People in their sixties, seventies and eighties embark on new careers, new pastimes and new relationships, and yet our existing cultural and social perceptions of ageing remain governed by increasingly dated images and narratives from a bygone era. This anthology challenges the stereotypes by bringing together eight previously unpublished stories of ordinary British people born between 1925 and 1945 that present contemporary ageing in a new light and show how the two generations that grew up with the founding of the Welfare State went on to experience much more than simply security from cradle to grave.

The anonymous diarists (the names used here are all pseudonyms) featured in this anthology can be divided in terms of a chronology of their birth related to the Second World War, and that divide can be argued to reflect in a broad sense the impact of historical events and how these were inflected in the respondents' overarching personal and sociocultural experiences and opinions, notwithstanding any differences arising from the variation within individual social circumstances. So the general classification structuring this collection is a marking out of the diarists and their lives in two discrete sections: the first being the interwar births and the second those born during wartime. While the diarists anthologized here are not a representative sample in a statistical sense, they do cover between them a wide range of social experience which is indicative of the general British experience of growing old in the Welfare State and suggestive of a generational difference between those who grew up in part before the Second World War and those born during it, who largely grew up in the post-1945 era. As a result of this generational difference, the narratives in *Growing Old with the Welfare State* collectively present an interesting multilayered account of a general social shift away from values rooted in the deference and social niceties of the pre-war period (some of which date back to the nineteenth century) to new, more informal, ways of living that began to appear from the late 1960s onwards.

Another consequence of the generational selection criteria for the inclusion of diarists in this book is that it enables comparison with the work of historians who have drawn on life writing from the Mass-Observation Archive. James Hinton's *Seven Lives from Mass Observation* (2016) focuses on seven mass observers born between the early 1920s and the early 1930s: 'Because the people dealt with here engaged with the defining transformations of the late twentieth century as adults, their sensibilities and expectations shaped by an earlier era, their experiences are particularly valuable in helping us to view those transformations in historical context' (4). Two of the mass observers included in *Growing Old with the Welfare State* (Dick Turpin and Beryl Saunders) are also featured (under different names) by Hinton in *Seven Lives* (and two more of Hinton's subjects make up the list of eight mass observers selected by Hubble in 2010 as potential FCMAP case studies from which the six included in *Growing Old with the Welfare State* were selected). There is something especially engaging about reading the thoughtful and detailed reflections of those who have lived through the significant social changes since the early 1930s which draws researchers to them. However, it is also fascinating to consider how that generation's attitudes were shaped by their relationship with the following generation born in the 1940s, who also lived through interesting times but with a different set of perspectives. As Claire Langhamer notes in *The English in Love* (2013), her history of love, marriage and the emotional revolution in the twentieth century, the Second World War can be seen as an 'emotional watershed': 'a period of rapid discontinuity out of which emerged a subtly different set of intimate relations embedded in, and expressive of, changed gender and social relations' (9). The pre-war boundaries between public and private crumbled and the younger generation developed very different expectations of emotional intimacy than those whose values had already been formed in the earlier period. According to Langhamer, this 'revolution' unfolded over several post-war decades culminating in the 1960s, which she views as not so much the age of sexual permissiveness but as a 'golden age of romance' (11) that included expectations of emotional and sexual intimacy within a desired ideal of companionate marriage. However, while the evolution of attitudes to sex and relationships was more gradual and nuanced than the stereotypical idea of the 'swinging sixties' allows, people's understanding – especially those of the older generation whose attitudes were formed before the war – was often shaped by exactly such popular stereotypes.

In places within *Growing Old with the Welfare State* it is perhaps possible to detect instances of a conservative nostalgia underpinning the attitudes of the older generation born in the interwar period, as well as a concern that those younger were gifted even more opportunities, especially educationally. One might speculate further that these differences are due in part to the different social and historical conditions of the diarists' early years. Those born between the wars suffered very different privations and anxieties from those born during the Second World War, given that they were conscious during their childhood, adolescence or early adulthood of both the deleterious social effects of the Great Depression and the impending threat of global conflict resuming. Then, during the war itself, this generation were aware of the physical damage and the deaths, creating an outlook that is quite different from those born later, who were merely children during that appalling struggle, some far too young to be fully conscious of its impact. The following chart marks out graphically that chronological and experiential divergence.

Individual	Year Born	Approx. Age during WW2
Interwar births		
George Borrows	1921	18–24
Margaret Christopher	1927	12–18
Dick Turpin	1930	9–15
Beryl Saunders	1931	9–15
Wartime births		
Joy Warren	1939	0–6
Doug Frendon	1942	0–3
Brenda Allen	1943	0–2
Joanna Woods	1943	0–2

It should be noted that two of these memoirists, 'Joy Warren' and 'Joanna Woods', are not MO diarists but U3A members who were involved in the FCMAP reading groups. Their accounts are taken from the biographical life histories such participants were asked to contribute to the project, although they are supplemented by some of their specific responses to the novels they were asked to read (see Appendix). The other six chapters draw on the responses of the selected MO diarists to various 'directives' sent out to them. However, the majority of all of these chapters draws on responses to three directives in particular: 'Winter 1992 Part 1: Growing Older', 'Autumn 2006 Part 3 Age' and 'Winter 2009 Part 2: Books and You' (see Appendix). What these three directives had in common with the life histories compiled by U3A reading group members is that they asked respondents to reflect on the different stages of their lives, and therefore both approaches reveal a wealth of material not only on ageing as a continual process but also on how attitudes are formed and shaped at different stages of life.

Some of the potential differences resulting from the social possibilities, familial setting milieu and dominant value systems which influence individuals at these different periods of their lives will be highlighted in more detail in the introductory sections to the two parts of this anthology. In particular, aspects of the diarists' life stories will be described which suggest that perhaps the most significant factor in the difference between the outlooks of individuals and generations lies within the complex dynamics of the attitudinal framework of the culture they encounter as children and young adults, which continues to reverberate throughout their lives. The Afterword at the end of the book will then reassess any difference between the two generations and draw general conclusions, as well as returning to the question of how such written reflections relate to the development of a fourth-age subjectivity.

Works Cited

Hinton, James. *Nine Wartime Lives: Mass-Observation and the Making of the Modern Self*. Oxford: Oxford University Press. 2010.

Hinton, James. *Seven Lives from Mass Observation*. Oxford: Oxford University Press. 2016.

Hubble, Nick and Philip Tew. *Ageing, Narrative and Identity: New Qualitative Social Research*. Basingstoke: Palgrave Macmillan. 2013.

Karpf, Anne. *How to Age*. Basingstoke: Macmillan. 2014.

Langhamer, Claire. *The English in Love: The Intimate Story of an Emotional Revolution*. Oxford: Oxford University Press. 2013.

Laslett, Peter. *A Fresh Map of Life*. Basingstoke: Macmillan. 1996 [1989].

Timmins, Nicholas. *The Five Giants: A Biography of the Welfare State*. Hammersmith: Fontana. 1996.

PART ONE

The Interwar Generation

1

Introducing the Interwar Generation

Significantly the first four respondents whose extracted diary entries appear in the following four chapters were all born in the period between the world wars. The first three manifest aspects of a nostalgic outlook, defining themselves by the values of the interwar and war years, bemused by the changing values after the 1960s. The last seems to be more in tune with what Clare Langhamer calls the emotional revolution of the mid-century years, detailing her relationships from a liberal perspective which also informs her perspective as a social worker. However, by 2008 she worries of the financial profligacy of the young, echoing at least implicitly a return of some of the values of her youth, complaining of rising house prices which make her feel complicit with the awful dynamics of the financial system in crisis, although insisting nevertheless: 'But most of us bought houses as homes not investments!'

Born in 1921, the oldest respondent featured in this volume, George Borrows, despite going to a grammar school, still reflects in the MO autumn 2001 directive: 'I had no opportunity to go to a university as I was not bright enough for a scholarship and my parents could not afford to support me'. In the winter 2008 directive he records that 'as a child it was instilled in me that debt should be avoided. If you want something, save up for it'. In the summer 2006 directive, despite his liberal stance ideologically he still reflects positively on certain British values and yet stating of his youth that he was well aware of the terrible poverty faced by relatives in the 1920s during his infancy:

Was I taught core values when I was at school in Britain? Not at school, at home by the family and old fashioned values they were, like always to show respect to my elders. Always remove my hat when entering some one's home. Never allow a lady to stand when I had a seat on a bus.

Working class families did not travel by car in those days. Women were to be respected. On no account did a man offer violence to women. Men who did so were not worthy to be called a man.

In 1936, he went to work, ruminating in autumn 1997, 'When I was 15, I obtained my first job in the local Town Hall. In congratulating me my father said "And it's a job with a pension." He had his own small business without one. Planning for the future was impressed on me even then!' As he writes in the spring 2010 directive, 'I was in the pre-war T.A. [Territorial Army],' which he joined in 1939, aged eighteen. He also remembers the war clearly, describing in the spring 1992 directive how his father lost his business during that period. In the autumn 2001 directive he notes: 'In 1945 I parachuted into lower Burma and organised levies for intelligence work and sabotage against the Japanese.' And elsewhere in the spring 1994 directive, he stresses his limited experience of bodies during the war, and according to his own account, he faced only one in seven years, although still he does recollect the callousness inculcated by the conflict towards the news of another death, entirely unmoved by the demise of a fellow soldier killed by the Japanese, an Anglo-Indian officer in Burma. As he records, he had an earlier familiarity with death, writing, 'my first experience of death was as a schoolboy aged about 8 or 9. A boy in our class died of scarlet fever' followed by another classmate at 11. George adds:

> I don't think I have ever had a fear of dying. During the war my greatest worry – when I was at risk in Burma – was that if I was killed my parents would never really know what had happened to me and I knew this would add very much to their grief.

Later, however, he recalls in the autumn 2000 directive a cousin killed during the war and notes three others who were all 'regular soldiers'. In winter 2008, responding to the world financial crisis, he says: 'Let us hope it doesn't take massive rearmament to reduce unemployment as happened in the 30s.' George concludes in the summer 2006 directive, despite his liberal outlook that core British values mean, one belief is 'to be wary of change – conservative until there is overwhelming evidence that change is in fact long overdue'. Another significant set of values affecting his attitude reflective of the period of his upbringing is found in the spring 1998 directive when he recollects the familial silence concerning sex. He remembers a girlfriend at eighteen (in 1939) whose breasts he fondled: 'I would love to have gone further but was not allowed to and the great fear in those days was having an illegitimate baby,' knowing little about contraception. In the summer 1990 directive he adds of his experience: 'I knew very little about women; with brother officers on leave I'd visited the Calcutta brothels to find out what women's anatomy was like and to make sure that if we got killed at least we'd "Had a woman."' He adds that post-war he lost a fiancée after being reticent about sex with a young woman who later met someone while sailing out to Singapore: 'Even at the age of 27 [1948] I thought that "nice" girls did not want sex unless they were married and I was very concerned about an illegitimate child.' He records in spring 1998 meeting a young woman in 1953 of whom he was keen: 'However she had a fiancé who was out in Singapore and I would have thought it dishonourable to have pinched another chap's girl.' He also concludes of the marriage vows that breaching them represents a betrayal: 'The state of society today would be much happier if people had remembered that – from the Royal Family upwards. [...] Society ought to be based on trust, honesty, integrity, on things of value, not sordid hole-in-corner liaisons just to gratify one's senses.' He adds while noting the pain caused by affairs that 'I am of the generation that had settled and had growing families before the liberation of the pill in the 60s gave freedom for a different kind of morality.' One might perhaps trace a touch of envy, although he reasserts a sense of moral probity and stability that he finds desirable. He adds in summer 1990 that 'because divorce is easy people take marriage far too lightly'.

Born an only child in 1927 to a father aged fifty-three and a forty-two-year-old mother, Margaret Christopher was aged twelve to eighteen during the war, before which, from the ages of six to eleven, she had attended a boarding school. Her life was relatively affluent, and middle class in its values, although she found growing up in the countryside stultifying in certain ways. In the spring 2012 directive those rural years are evoked strongly by a photograph of her parents she reconsiders and which she had taken aged twelve. The same album featured a picture of their servants: 'They all look jolly and happy and were with us for years. By today's standards it was such a primitive world these pictures represented. I often think of it now that I have become old and feel almost a piece of history.' And, in spring 1992 she recalls that '[as] a country person, the shooting of pheasants, pigeons, rabbits and wild duck for food, especially during the war, provided the most down to earth illustration of the fact that we who are not vegetarians must kill to eat'. She adds:

> You might think that, growing up during war I would be affected by the casualties of battle and bombing raids. But only one cousin was killed in action, and he not one I knew well. And of course then, all descriptions of wartime events were verbal and not visual, thus less graphic.

Much like George Borrows, she too reflects on an unease with cultural attitudes and behaviour in the autumn 1998 directive (having herself survived breast cancer treatment in 1990), saying: 'Although seriously dismayed about a number of aspects of modern life, because I can choose how to conduct my own I enjoy my days and my work and I feel this must have a bearing on my good health.' Having grown up in Wales, she recollects in the autumn 2000 directive that her family rarely visited relatives, but:

> this changed during the war when at various times we sheltered several younger relatives, my mother's twin sister, her daughter, and later a cousin. Along with all the problems of living in the country with food and petrol rationing and the difficulties of running a large estate except for one clerk (he was a land agent), this was a severe strain for my father.

Her response to her father's death at which she was present when he was aged seventy-two in 1946 features in the spring 1994 directive, where she describes its suddenness, her devastation, her response in being physically sick, the loss of the house that was tied to his job and her estrangement from her mother. In autumn 2000 she again records his death, detailing how as a consequence she lost touch with his relatives in Yorkshire, including his seven brothers and sisters and their offspring, apart from a theatrically inclined aunt in Pinner whom she visited frequently after marrying in 1950 and relocating to London. She reflects: 'My parents and I were very much products of that distant past when stiff upper lips and carefully controlled emotions, at least in public, were the norm, partly I suppose because we had servants and one mustn't be undignified in front of them.' Nevertheless, in spring 2012, she recollects that 'my father loved the late Victorian music halls and very occasionally when he felt happy he would sing snatches of songs by Marie Lloyd and others; but my mother had felt it a handicap in her youth not to be able to play the piano at all well, or to sing'. She remembers playing the Blue Danube waltz on a wind-up gramophone, which 'seemed to hint at exotic worlds for which I longed, deep in rainy, wartime rural Wales'. In the summer 2011 directive, thinking of her mother's death alone in hospital on Christmas Eve when Margaret was herself forty-two, she admits that 'I look back with shame on my neglect of my mother in her old age. I was her only child and should have been aware of how much help and support she needed; but somehow I never grasped what is now obvious to me'.

As she relates in autumn 2000 after divorce in around 1980, her more prosperous relative, 'my mother's niece, who is single, has given me £24,000 when I most needed it to buy a house I now live in with my daughter'. She is bemused by the child-centric aspects of contemporary culture:

> My mother was a very loving person, but clueless when it came to child-rearing and I suspect her mother must have been the same. I myself didn't take happily to motherhood because children are so totally self-centred for the first few years and although I made huge self-denials for my

husband in terms of the way we lived our lives, I didn't, and still can't see why children today are so much the centre of attention. Secretly I believe (as my brother-in-law used to say) that they should be 'seen and not heard,' and that their lives should fit with ours rather than the other way round.

While worrying about the impact of circumstances on her own pension and savings, in winter 2008, she reacts to the world financial crisis, labelling it a *recession*, and comments: 'Being a frugal person who has never taken any form of loan, I look on financiers who made their piles by tempting financially innocent people into taking loans and mortgages they could not afford with loathing. [...]. Older people who haven't grown up with the idea of instant gratification do find it easier to resist temptations.'

In autumn 2001, she deplores the Americanization of the media, with its 'gossip about totally uninteresting people, consumerism, waste, greed, "spin," false values and everything which is contributing to the ruin of the world as people of my generation knew it'. She adds of the mass media or 'gutter press' that 'they seem to pander to the two saddest trends (after "political correctness") "dumbing down" and fostering a short attention span by discussing nothing at length or in depth', opining the focus on greed and sensationalism. She notes that even Radio 4's *Today* programme indulges in 'sound bites!' rather than extended coverage. In winter 2008 she blames American malls, consumerism and overproduction for contributing to the world financial crisis, citing evidence that both food and resources more generally are being wasted wilfully, again blaming the media for 'spreading the culture of greed'. In winter 2009 she objects to the culture the media fosters in putting oneself first, which in the case of women is leading to the 'destruction of family life in the process'. In spring 2012 she opines people's disinterestedness in any concept such as the Big Society, their lack of involvement socially and politically.

> Discounting myself as too old to be involved, take my daughter who, at 60 is active and fit but completely uninterested in doing any formal voluntary work or taking an active part in community policy-making. My younger grand-daughter, age 24, when asked if she would vote in the forthcoming mayoral elections declared herself to be totally uninterested in politics. This is of course very worrying for the long term.

Despite her liberal values, membership of CND from 1958, work with seekers of asylum at a Citizens Advice Bureau in London, and four years as committee member and company secretary for a West Indian Pensioners' club, in autumn 2001 she concludes: 'Now, any discussion of race is a minefield, largely dominated by political correctness, which means dispassionate colloquy is virtually impossible,' a fact she attributes to blaming colonialism for all current problems, before deciding that the post-war media 'was much more "responsible" than it is today'. In spring 1998 she admits an affair for a year during her marriage with a 'reckless, irresponsible' formerly bisexual younger builder which she admits her then husband found painful, as she did when her husband had sex with a house guest who had visited them when they lived in France. Nevertheless she writes: 'What puzzles me about the modern attitude to sex is what appears to be a total lack of any connection between it and tenderness, let alone romantic love,' still regarding sex as a *sacred, almost mystical act*. On a personal level in spring 1992 she states that 'I never replace anything (except clothes) because it has become dated!' – a clear rejection of current consumerism for its own sake. And in spring 1994 she suggests that contemporary society respects very little, neither the living nor even the dead, and she concludes that 'I see the world in Manichean terms of good and evil forces, with evil uppermost throughout most of this century'.

Born in Tottenham in 1930, moving to Enfield in 1937, Dick Turpin was aged nine to fifteen during the war years and, at the outbreak, was on holiday in Stockport with paternal grandparents where he remained for three years. At this time Dick in the spring 2012 directive remembers listening to Gracie Fields's songs 'Sing as You Go' and 'The Biggest Aspidistra in the World' on a wind-up gramophone. His father was directed to war work in Dartford, where the family including Dick joined him in 1942.

When reflecting on death in the spring 1994 directive he describes one consequence of having been born so soon after the First World War as growing up with a sense of the solemnity of the two-minute silence on Armistice Day and the sense of loss accompanying that. Remembering the newsreel footage of the liberation of Belsen, he adds that 'when the Second World War began I was soon aware of man's seemingly endless capacity for mass slaughter'. In 2012 he recalls 'singing solo in the 1940 carol service. It was the night Hitler blitzed Manchester'. In the autumn 2000 directive he remembers the many moves in childhood until the end of the war, attending five different schools. However, 'after the war just as it seemed we were settled in our home at Enfield [in 1944], north of London, my mother got the urge to open a guest house in Brighton. A notion that was not at all popular with the rest of the family'. His father moved to a job in Hayward's Heath, Sussex, and in 1949 they moved to Brighton which he disliked, so, aged nineteen, Dick joined the army for five years to support himself. After military service (during which his brother committed suicide, aged twenty in 1956), Dick married in 1957, aged twenty-seven, having remained celibate until the night of his wedding. The couple had three sons born in 1957, 1959 and 1962. He frequently confirms his home life has been happy, believing faithfulness being important to a marriage's well-being, although he does admit in autumn 2000 that his 'by the standards of to-day [was] not very prosperous'. He regards the younger generation as irresponsible, identifying several root causes, one of which was changes to education:

> Another difficult age began when my sons started at school, in the early sixties. A time when so-called progressive and enlightened ideas had begun to dominate education and teaching, Ideas that were a total disaster and are indeed the cause of so many social problems today. Mine was a constant battle with trendy head teachers and an educational establishment that was failing to teach my sons the basic rules of mathematics or how to write a simple letter.

He records the loss of his middle son, aged twenty, who was knocked off a motorcycle in France by a drunken driver, as leaving a *permanent scar* and making him angry at the lenient *joke sentence*. He details his surviving sons' divorces and failed relationships, suggesting, 'the young women they have partnered have been truly incredible, irresponsible beyond belief', living on debts and claiming almost every one of his generation known to him has had to bail out their offspring financially. He believes women must shoulder much of the burden of responsibility and argues that feminism has led mothers to neglect their children. He argues that fault should still be judged regarding divorce, because there is still the reality of so much suffering and loss for the *innocent party*. He concludes that happiness still eludes women pursuing a feminist agenda, citing not only the case of his sons but also that of his nephews. However, he sees signs their own sons are increasingly unsympathetic to their mothers: 'When his stepfather makes the mother of my oldest grandson cry his response is, "She married him," and evicted his father from the family home to do it.' He also believes people have no shame regarding illegitimacy, adultery and even criminal behaviour, quite unlike the past when *misdemeanours* were *hushed up*. In autumn 2001, as regards the mass media, he believes they do not reflect either his life or opinions and that they exploit sex to boost their appeal, and he reflects that 'the thought of a media diet of *Coronation Street*, *EastEnders*, and *The Weakest Link* fills me with dread'. He also reports being tired of the *yah-boo* debate in politics and hating spin doctors. Having worked in local government for over thirty years in Worthing, he notes few councillors were poor and, in his opinion, incompetent. He reflects on having been an active socialist in his youth but never having had much faith in the Labour Party. As an active unionist, he felt trades unions should have remained impartial politically: 'Sadly union bosses would not hear of it. More interested in gongs and other perks.' He argues those who regard older people as a burden are not reflecting an accurate picture, adding 'almost all the younger relations I have make far more demands of the N.H.S.

than I do. Perhaps, it is because, growing up in wartime, we did not have the same expectations that the young have today.' Identifying a rot beginning in the *swinging sixties*, he also states the many of the younger generation take on too much debt, neglect their health through smoking, are both sexually irresponsible and generally too dependent on the welfare state.

> Many of today's problems just did not exist when I was young. Girls just did not consent to casual sex. Well nice girls didn't. Life was so much simpler. [...] I was brought up to stand on my own two feet, pay my bills, owe nothing to anyone. I would never have thought of buying a car on credit. As a man I was always taught to respect women.

In spring 1994 he blames much of what he regards as a contemporary malaise on the welfare state and modern education with its enlightened and progressive ideas and says: 'Society used to respect the dead; that is certainly not the case today,' saddened that his son's grave has been vandalized on three occasions and aggrieved by members of the younger generation with their 'abuse of war memorials'. He suggests: 'The idea was sown that children represented the future and must be denied nothing. I dubbed my sons and their school friends the "I want" generation,' concluding they had subsequently gone on to fail as parents because of endless *self-gratification*, which has undermined the *sanctity* of marriage as an institution. He suggests that his working world of local government was punctuated by numerous infidelities, including many of his superiors, which affected delivery of services deleteriously:

> Equally, I found that subordinate staff with too much interest in crumpet were just as unreliable. Whoever claims that a person's moral conduct is of no importance so long as they do their job well is a Pratt! A person capable of ratting on their spouse and family is capable of ratting on anyone.

As an instinctive conservative, Dick is against legal abortion apart from where the mother's life is endangered, and generally he regards affairs and casual affairs as a negative and corrosive element of contemporary culture and compares it negatively with the past. He notes: 'Both my wife and myself grew up with loving and caring parents, who in their time, between two world wars had to overcome many hardships and difficulties, such as to-day's young people would find hard to even imagine,' later identifying 'a generation of young people ever ready to assert their rights but with no interest in their obligations'. Blaming Thatcherite greed and manipulation as the causes of the dynamics of the credit crunch, and identifying Blair as a Thatcherite, Dick Turpin records the opinion in winter 2008 that 'contrary to popular belief, ordinary people in this country have never been that prosperous. Specially those of us who grew up before, or in the early days of the welfare state. My wife had had a lifetime's experience of frugal shopping. For her it is as natural as breathing'. In summer 1990 he records positively other values of his youth, recollecting that 'in those days if a young man got a girl "into trouble" he was expected to marry her and support his offspring', blaming promiscuity and the permissive society for social problems and unhappiness, suggesting 'such attitudes' have contributed nothing to in enhancing the *quality of life in Britain*, rather introducing a 'decline in moral integrity'.

Born in 1931, Beryl Saunders was aged nine to fifteen during the war, but it seemed relatively distant as she grew up in a small seaside town in West Dorset. In spring 1992 she described her mother's life:

> I find it hard to imagine what my mother did with her time when I was small, before the 1939–45 war. In an ordinary 3-bedroomed house she had a maid who worked full-time, living in – the maid got up by 7 and did the breakfast – then spent about half the morning doing the cleaning, the other half getting lunch.

This changed with the outbreak of hostilities, causing great stress for her mother in a period which she describes in autumn 2000 as having 'brought about a complete change in my parent's life. Things were very grim at home – there always seemed to be babies screaming and my parents were very short-tempered.…perhaps this led to.…' She recalls in spring 1998 on a directive concerned with having affairs of a family secret in her early years:

> Such relationships were still spoken about in a whisper, behind closed doors, shocking. We didn't know what 'adultery' meant till we reached our teens. Yet my family was quite considerably rattled by a quasi-affair of my father's: muttered about, hinted about, never pronounced openly.
>
> My father had an intense, loving relationship with a girl in his office during the late war years; she was a close family friend – still is. She was at my father's death-bed in 1979. Whether their relationship was a sexual one, we shall never know (unless she takes me into her confidence pretty soon). It caused plenty of gossip in our small town, plenty of anger towards my father on the part of my mother's sisters and friends.

In winter 2008 Beryl reports her mother's menopause at fifty which was symptomless apart from her periods ceasing 'much to her relief – she dreaded another pregnancy, having produced two children in her forties'. In autumn 2000 she ruminates that 'I experience the same ambivalence during the rare phone conversations or correspondence with my brother and sister. I rarely feel on the same wavelength, *except when face to face*. [...] We are very, very different [...] did we really issue from the same parents, a conventional middle-class couple' (emphasis in original). She recalls in 1990 the prohibitions on masturbation as a child in the 1930s and vividly recollects crushes in her teens with peers and for older girls in the 1940s at her Church of England *fairly repressive* girls' school. She comments: 'Sex for schoolgirls in the 1940s was sexual intercourse which happened to you for the first time on your wedding night and was feared, or [which] very bad unmarried girls did with American soldiers.' In autumn 2000 she adds of her parents that 'I only fell out with them seriously during parts of my teens. I was more intelligent and bookish than them, which was a frequent cause of friction'.

Also in autumn 2000 Beryl confesses that she was expelled from her exclusive boarding school in 1948 halfway through the Sixth Form for poor grades, her father unwilling to make up the scholarship fees, and as she writes: 'Of course I knew *nobody must ever know*.' Later that year she left home to work in Bristol, and in 1953, she was married, aged twenty-two, to an accountant five years older than her (both still virgins at the time). They went on to have a son and daughter. She recalls in the fifties you could visit a family planning clinic a few weeks before nuptials but were still addressed as *Mrs*. In spring 1992 she recalls nostalgically the free time her marriage allowed her, saying of visits to London and local Adult Education classes, 'this was a time when the pace of life was definitely in my favour', although clearly she had earlier more resented its failings. As she reflects in 2008, she and her husband split up in 1971, after which she qualified as a social worker. The final divorce came in 1974, and in 1990 she admitted she had found the reality of separating upsetting, blaming the failings on her naivety in marrying when so young. Both had had affairs, but her husband never suspected hers and the later divorce was acrimonious, the children feeling bewildered and abandoned. Her parents were initially in denial over the divorce, and 'when they did take it in they were so ashamed they never told any of their friends – for years'. Of her children she revels in their teens, admitting 'I must be honest and say I almost enjoyed a second teens myself and that there was still an element of anger, rebellion, and "I'll show you" in my behaviour'. In spring 1998 she confessed to a *relationship à trois*:

Some 15 years ago a woman friend of long standing left her husband to live with a new partner – also separated. They invited me to share sex with them. I found I hated leaving them together afterwards – we'd been so close it was like leaving loving parents. Also I found myself intensely attracted to my friend's partner – once or twice we continued our sexual activity after she got up early to go to work.

During the subsequent post-divorce eighteen years, she records fourteen love affairs, one of which was the reason she moved north to Yorkshire in 1979, taking a job near her married lover, forcing her twenty-two-year-old son into virtual homelessness. After a period of intense isolation during which her father died, she met a younger gardener who moved in with her after coming as a bed and breakfast guest, but even in 1990 she felt unable to tell her mother, brother or sister who she believed are 'old-fashioned' and would have expected her to remarry. She adds, 'I imagine I'm typical of one aspect of my generation. I discovered love and sex outside marriage pretty late,' dismissing friends with the same partner since the 1950s as 'very set in their ways'. However, elsewhere in her response she admits to the loneliness she suffered when single, with Sundays *the worst day of the week*, the day on which her separated daughter now rings her. 'I can tell she just can't work out a way of restructuring Sunday as a person in her own right.' In 1990, speaking as a social worker, she concedes the problems of serial relationships, seeing the dark side of successive 'Daddies' with children confused, partners trying to compensate for loneliness regardless of the effect on their offspring. She reflects on the changes from the past:

> When my parents married my Mum didn't know what my Dad earned. She STILL didn't know what he earned or the exact amount of his pension when he died 50+ years later!!! She never worked – yet her pension from his contributions from his employment is still more than mine will be when I retire having worked 20 years in local government. Marriage no longer offers 'security' or status to a woman.

She would not oppose gay marriage but finds the emphasis on gay rights off-putting. And she concludes in autumn 2009 that 'attitudes and expectations about what constitutes family life, what constitutes a relationship are simply a world away from the family I came into in 1931'.

In 1990, in an amused tone, she records her own mother's desire to see her grandchildren married, citing 'a blistering letter' sent to her daughter when she began living with her boyfriend. In 1998 she discusses situations where affairs are damaging, especially 'where vulnerable people are hurt, betrayed and damaged' citing financial loss, disruption to children and *the web of deceit* which erodes trust. And in autumn 2000 she describes their concern for her brother after being bereaved regarding 'his haphazard choice of companions' which dissipated when he remarried a neighbour, also opines her own lack of grandchildren and admits her relationship is difficult, her partner shifting without cause from emotional warmth to being 'suddenly monstrously angry, cold, taciturn, critical of everything'. She looks back with nostalgia to the time spent alone, admitting: 'Just recently I have been very unhappy, but see no way of putting things right. Any attempt at discussion he describes as nagging.' Much earlier she had vowed to never cheat on her new partner and, now suffering from failing eyesight, writing on the credit crunch in winter 2008, she describes having cleared her mortgage and her own aversion to credit cards. Describing her daughter and husband as accustomed 'to a bon viveur, credit based life-style; they are seriously addicted to shopping', she insists too that 'debt multiplies'. Reflecting on herself and her partner, she concludes: 'We simply manage on what we have. You'll hear similar reports from many of my generation,' thus aligning herself firmly with certain values of her youth, the make-do-and-mend spirit of wartime on most issues.

These attempts to describe and highlight how aspects of the attitudinal framework, of the culture the diarists encountered as children and young adults, continued to reverberate throughout their lives point to the shared persistence of certain values that might be considered small 'c' conservative. Interestingly, Hinton (2016) identifies five of his seven mass observers (with the diarist here called Beryl Saunders being one of the exceptions) as becoming 'drawn to the right in British politics' (163), with no less than three of them (including the diarist we call Dick Turpin) becoming attracted to varying degrees to the United Kingdom Independence Party (UKIP). Such political identifications are not always given a three-dimensional depth in public discourse. One of the advantages of the following chapters, compiled from the diarists' own accounts originally written for Mass Observation, is that these detailed and self-reflective life histories afford us some insight into how these various conservative (and other) cultural values continue to have impact throughout lives lived across sustained and, in some cases, paradigmatic social change.

Work Cited

Hinton, James. *Seven Lives from Mass Observation*. Oxford: Oxford University Press. 2016.

2

'I Never Stopped Learning All My Life'

George Borrows

George Borrows *was born in 1921 and is now in his nineties. He is very happily married and has four children. He moved from Lancashire to South England in 1984 after retiring from his job as a senior executive of an international manufacturing company and now lives in Chichester, West Sussex. George served in the army for seven years from the age of eighteen, spending periods in Burma, India and British Guiana (including a stint in tropical logging operations) before being hospitalized with tuberculosis for a year. His time in the army and working in isolated jungles left him feeling naive about women, and his early romantic relationships were a learning experience. After two failed engagements, George married 'late' at the age of thirty-three when he fell in love with a widowed night sister while ill in hospital.*

George feels positive about growing older and thinks there are 'tremendous compensations on reaching retirement age and beyond'. After retiring, he travelled the world for five months and took up sailing as a pastime. He also became heavily involved with the local cathedral. He enjoys being able to dictate the pace of life in old age: 'The fever of my life is over though I feel fit enough to do whatever work I'm called upon to do … I have a happy home and a peace which I often wonder what I've done to deserve.' As a very active person, George has also been involved in volunteer work and studied philosophy through a WEA course. He now considers himself a 'Deist' after questioning Christianity, his former faith. George survived a 'moderately severe' heart attack in his early seventies and currently struggles with his vision and osteoarthritis. He receives domestic help and uses a stick and scooter. He worries about his wife outliving him and wants to function as independently as possible. Retaining his possessions is essential in this respect. George reflects extensively on death and dying and recalls his 'sense of relief' when his ageing grandfather passed away. He has critical views on government policy and pensions. He considers the ageing population – particularly the large numbers who suffer from poverty and loneliness – to be a significant social problem.

Aside from the three main directives discussed in the introduction and appendix of this book, the material in this chapter is also taken from replies to the following MO directives: 1994 'Death and Bereavement', 1998 'Staying Well and Everyday Life', 2001 'Media and the Public Interest' and 2011 'Ageing and Care'.

Winter 1992, aged 70: I took a generous offer for early retirement ten years ago, and have been able to dictate the pace of things ever since. Life has never been better. I put work behind me the day that I left and have never missed any of what I did in the past. I had a number of demanding jobs, and looking back, I marvel at some of the things that I found time to do, and look with some regret at the priorities I sometimes chose.

Even with hindsight I don't see how I could have done much differently. Being given a drive to achieve things I could not have done less at work, and some sort of outside voluntary work was a necessary contribution to the community, but it made me less patient with my children than I ought to have been and I don't feel we had much fun together. We had good holidays and so on, but home life suffered through my lack of time for them. For a whole year I was busy laying out a new garden in a new house – laying paving, bricklaying to make raised flowerbeds, digging a pond, making a pergola – if I'd just put it all down to grass I expect the kids would have been happier and I'd have had more time with them.

Having married late – I was thirty-five – there is more than the average difference in my attitude to them. When I was in my twenties I got on well with other people's children, but I found by the time I was fifty that I became bored with their interests: we have one grandchild at the moment whom we see only once or twice a year, and even now when I have the time to give to her I cannot raise much enthusiasm for playing with her.

I cannot find it in my prayer-book to check the exact wording, but there is a prayer which beautifully sums up the way I feel about life now.

Protect us O Lord all the day long of this troublous life, until the shades lengthen, the evening comes, the busy world is hushed, the fever of life is over and our work is done. Then Lord in thy mercy grant us safe lodging, holy rest and peace at the last.

The fever of my life is over, though I feel fit enough to do whatever work I'm called upon to do. I'm involved in various voluntary activities which I conduct at my own pace, I have a happy home and a peace which I often wonder what I've done to deserve.

I am seventy-two in May. I have never thought of myself as anything more than 'middle-aged', but I expect anyone else would call me elderly at least (though I think I am being realistic in thinking that only someone very young would look on me as 'old'). Certainly many people of about my own age are kind enough to express surprise when I tell them my age.

My poor assessment of age can be illustrated when I was sailing this last summer. I was clearly the eldest member of the crew of eight, but one chap I looked upon as a near-contemporary. When I asked him about his war-time experiences he look[ed] hurt and said he had done his National Service in the 1950s. I don't look at people specifically in terms of their age so I make no assumptions on that basis. Talk of the sixties generation, for example, means nothing to me – I cannot work out if there is anyone I know in that generation. That is the time when three of my four children were born, but I'd never think of classifying them as belonging to a particular generation.

I think it does a person an injustice if you think about their age as a separate part of their identity. I meet people in a wide age-band both when sailing – my hobby – and in my Church activities, and apart from thinking, 'He's younger than I am' or 'she's about my age', I don't automatically put an age on to them. I couldn't do that with any accuracy at all.

A couple of weeks before Xmas I went to a lunch given by my old employer for retired senior managers to meet their old colleagues. It was fun to see people whom I had known, and in some cases developed as young managers, now in the company's top positions. I do not go every year as it is a 500-mile round trip, so in some cases I was not sure whether the person I was speaking to was working or retired. A good rule of thumb was that the worried ones were working and the carefree ones with a good sun tan were the pensioners. In fact, it is the fifty and sixty-year-olds that I feel sorry for – I can visualize the stresses of running a company in these times and I tell them all to retire as soon as they can. I've never regretted for a moment that I had an opportunity to go at sixty-one instead of sixty-three.

I enjoy the company of people of my own age and have quite a few friends like that. I also have some now in their eighties, so I can see what time is likely to bring me. One, who is a retired ambassador, is [turning] ninety next month and he still lives alone; mentally very alert but very frail. He was sailing with me until about six years ago, but I know he finds life a struggle and has confessed that he has considered suicide if it drags on too long.

I still have a good head of hair – not long ago I was a bit upset to be told it was grey; I'd always looked upon it as brown! But even at the age of fifty or so my elder daughter used to tease me about my receding hair line as I developed a 'higher forehead'. I always feel I have an edge on people much younger than I am who have large bald patches!

I don't know how the ageing process affects women in general. My wife has the same lapses of memory as I do, we can keep up with each other when we walk and still enjoy sex together, tho' not as frequently as I'd like. My old ambassador friend lost most of his zest for life when he could no longer get an erection. Having lost his wife some years ago, he had a number of lady-friends, some of whom I am sure gave him all the encouragement that they could. I think men have an advantage at my age as at almost any function – evening classes, church, theatre, parties and so on there are always two unattached women for every man. Another very old friend's wife left him some ten years ago. He now had a very attractive companion who is about twenty years younger.

I think there are tremendous compensations in reaching retirement age and beyond. I have no ambitions to drive me, no real worries (except major ones like the kind of world I shall leave to my grandchildren) and can do as much as I please or have time to stand and stare.

Physically of course one has lots of limitations – I used to walk on the fells, Pennine Way and so on when I was in my fifties; now there are too many aching joints to deter one from more than a couple of hours' gentle stroll. When I'm sailing I find that the younger members of the crew tactfully arrange for the less arduous tasks to fall my way.

So far as a favourite age is concerned I think it must be now – I am free of care, which as long as one is working of bringing up a family is always present. Life has been very good to me – I don't know that I ever had expectations; though I had hopes and ambitions. My ambitions – in the sense of obtaining particular positions in various jobs I have had – have not been fulfilled at times, but then it was probably better for me that they were not.

Are there any things I would have done differently? ... One of the things I would have learned to do would be to have held my tongue on many occasions. I remember reading once a remark (probably meant cynically or humorously, I can't remember) about a man who 'never said anything to hurt anyone, except those whom he loved'. I can look back to times when I have said things I have bitterly regretted, arrogant or humiliating, to my grandmother, mother and wife.

The good point about care for the elderly in general is that one doesn't hear of old people being homeless, so someone looks after them. The bad point is that, from what one sees on some TV programmes, the old sit around like cabbages in a circle while someone with an out-of-tune piano tries to get them to single 'It's a long way to Tipperary'.

I don't think we respect the old anymore than we respect any other group of people – the people sleeping on the streets, the unemployed, the deprived, the people who travel by bus because they can't afford a car, people who read *The Sun* because they can't read words of more than two syllables, politicians – you name it, we'll show disrespect for it!!

1994, aged 73: When I was almost fifteen my Grandfather died. He had always lived with us as he lost his wife when he was only about sixty-four and my mother was his eldest daughter. He taught me draughts, chess, [and] cribbage and was always on hand to baby-sit for my parents. Not that they went out much – a weekly visit to the cinema was about the limit of their social life.

I had to share a bedroom with Grandpa for much of my boyhood and always remember him coming to bed and kneeling for his prayers. In his eighties he became rather confused, and when he was particularly difficult my father became annoyed with him – about the only time I can remember him being really irritable. In his final, short illness I was moved to another room and my mother slept in my bed. He died in the middle of the night and my mother woke me to go to let her sister know. She lived right at the other side of the town and I enjoyed the cycle ride through the deserted streets. While I was getting dressed I remember my mother just saying in a very broken voice: 'Oh, father'. I don't know how much grief she felt – it must have been mixed with relief.

On the day of the funeral I was messing about before assembly at school and a pal said, 'I wouldn't have thought you'd be behaving like this when it's your grandad's funeral', and I replied, 'It's not something you have to feel bad about'. Partly this was to indicate the sense of relief that the tensions that had existed at home had disappeared, but also because I was in a church choir – as was the boy who spoke to me – and I think I was trying to show that what the church taught meant something to me. My cousin was there and I think I shocked him a little as being unfeeling, but he did not realize what it was like to have a slightly demented old man living with you all the time. My mother always slightly resented that her younger sister took no responsibility for her father.

Though I was in the Army for seven years, right through the war I was in contact with a body only once. There was an accidental shooting in the guardroom on a site in India and I had to go down when I heard the alarm. I saw the body on the floor and had to make sure he was dead, which meant opening the shirt and looking at the wound and feeling for a heartbeat. The other officer who had followed me said afterwards, 'I couldn't have done that', and I remember saying: 'I could only do it because I had to with others looking on'.

There were four of us in a long-range penetration group behind the Japanese lines in Burma, organizing local levies and gathering intelligence. One was an Anglo-Indian officer: he did not appear so and I remember being surprised to find that he's never been to the U.K. At one time we had to split up and it was not till later that we regrouped and I heard that John had been surprised and killed by the Japanese. None of us three survivors felt too deeply about it: it was rather a callous time.

I have had a very good life and would rather die in my sleep tonight than live to be confused and incontinent in ten or so years' time. Lots of people have died already; if my belief in a continued consciousness is wrong and there is merely oblivion, I shall know nothing about it so won't be able to worry. If there is a new existence it will be very exciting and may be even better than the one on this earth. I can't imagine many old people being pleased with their bodies; creaky, wrinkled, skin blemishes, unresponsive to request for effort. I look at mine and think that it won't be a bad thing to get rid of it in the crematorium one day.

Autumn 1996, aged 77: Years ago, and I can't remember where, I came across the advice 'Live as if you are going to die tomorrow; plan as if you are going to live to 100'. Excellent advice, which I have tried to follow and have no regrets in having done so.

I finished [my working life] as head of the world-wide Group Pensions Department. I had a wide arena in which to work at a time when the Labour Government was bringing in the State Earnings Related Pension Scheme – an admirable contribution towards solving the problem of caring for people in their old age, which could have been developed still further as time went by. To our shame and loss, subsequent governments have decided that we could not afford it and are now struggling to find suitable alternatives. In the interim the Tories set up 'private pensions', which whilst suitable for a minority of mobile people, enabled unscrupulous salesmen to sell expensive [and] utterly unsuitable schemes to ignorant, gullible people.

I was thirty-eight when I joined my last employer and until then was in a poor pension fund. I was married with a family and glad that I could join a scheme which would provide for them if I died [...] Thirty-eight is leaving it quite late so I paid extra contributions as I could afford them – at one time contributing directly and indirectly some twenty percent of my net pay. As a result of planning I have already had sixteen years of very comfortable retirement, and when I die my wife will have no financial problems either.

It goes deeper of course – living as if one is going to die tomorrow means not leaving too many loose ends, unfinished business that ought to be settled. And in family relationships, 'not letting the sun go down on one's wrath'. I've not always succeeded but it has been worth the effort.

I look forward with interest and no trepidation to Death. It may seem inconsistent, but I will have a Christian funeral. A proper ceremony for such an occasion is necessary for those left behind. I hope that there will be a choir so that S. S. Wesley's anthem 'Thou wilt keep him in perfect peace, whose mind is stayed on thee' can be sung. That puts my uncertain feelings into perspective.

It may sound a cynical point of view, but I reason that at death we either retain a sense of our own identity in another life – in which case it will be an interesting challenge (provided my problem with 'eternity' is resolved!) – or there is oblivion, in which case we are not even aware of its happening and have nothing to worry about. We shan't even be able to say: 'What a pity I have wasted so much time listening to sermons on Sundays'. Whatever happens to our remains, the individual atoms which make up our bodies ... will be incorporated into some other product of nature. Matter is indestructible and our bodies will be recycled – perhaps that is what is meant by eternity?

1998, aged 77: [F]or sixteen years I have been a pensioner.

We moved to this flat five years ago, having realized that even the small garden which we then had would eventually be more than we could manage.

We were very active when we first retired. A six-month trip round the world, a four-month caravan tour around Spain and Portugal, many continental motoring holidays and weekend breaks. I took up sailing, passed my RYA examinations and had my own boat for some years (my wife refused to set foot in it after 'it moved' when she stepped onto it from the jetty on her first visit of inspection!! She has never been a sailor). In my boat, and with friends in other yachts, I have sailed along most of the South Coast, the Channel Isles and on to Shetland and Norway. All in ten years or so of a new hobby – one which I had always wanted to be able to do without any opportunity – in the early years of retirement. It looks as if I was fit.

Then five years ago (just after we moved into this flat, after fifteen months of trying to sell our house, which might be significant) I had a moderately severe heart attack. My heart is damaged, but that of itself would not have restricted my activities so much had my constitution been a bit stronger. During the war, and then as a civilian, I spent in all some eleven years in the tropics. In Burma I had had malaria two or three times, jaundice and dysentery and various skin problems. Then in 1954, whilst working in the forests in Guyana, I was diagnosed with T.B. and spent eighteen months getting over lung surgery and a spinal infection. Lying on my back for six months led to bowel problems and years later I had to have surgery for diverticulitis. However, it is the restricted breathing plus the damaged heart which sap my vitality now.

I still try to be active – I do voluntary work at the Cathedral, tho' I have given most of it up – but after a couple of hours on my feet I really need to sit down.

Quite deliberately we chose a flat with a lift. We are on the top floor because of the view – and I always use it to come up, though walking down is no problem (except when the Synovitis in my hip joint is playing up!) My inabilities annoy me, but because of my wife's eye problems they do not greatly affect our daily lives as she is compelled to stay indoors most of the time. She will eventually lose almost all her sight and in the mean time sunlight causes her a lot of pain.

I have never obtained any enjoyment from 'keeping fit' by any special regime or exercises or jogging ... My weight has never exceed 145 lbs, and I am 5' 9" tall, so I can forget about it and eat what I like, though we have always eaten a very healthy diet; my wife would be a vegetarian (as is one of my daughters) if it were not for the fact that I enjoy meat. We have a bottle of wine with our evening meal and make it last two evenings. At lunch I have a Guinness and my wife a small can of beer. With gin, sherry, port or malt whiskey in reasonable quantities we comfortably fall within the recommended alcohol intake. My short-term memory worries me but everyone of my age that I speak to complains about the same problem.

2001, aged 80: I read the *Guardian* news, comment and leader pages fairly thoroughly everyday and go to their excellent website if I want to pick up some additional detail. I started reading the paper in India in 1943 when it arrived in bundles of half a dozen by sea, anything from a month to two months old (and sometimes in the wrong order!). It came to me from an aunt, and I never discovered why because she was a terrible Tory all her life. Maybe she hoped to wean me gradually from my reading of the *Tribune* and the *New Statesman*! Anyhow at a young and impressionable age – I had no opportunity to go to a university as I was not bright enough for a scholarship and my parents could not afford to support me – it helped form opinions which have lasted me throughout my life. They must have been convincing, as my children, and my wife who came from a Tory family, are all as deep-dyed liberals as I am.

Being a full and active member of a democratic society should mean taking the trouble to be informed about matters of local and national interest and when an issue is important enough to you, taking some action. I have written numerous letters to MPs, the *Guardian* and my local paper about things I feel strongly about, and I took part recently in a march to protest about the American bombing of Afghanistan.

Reform of government and the Lords and the abolition of the monarchy are things which are unlikely to happen in my time, unfortunately. The local government reforms still fail to give power down at the level where the people affected can make decisions; even on issues which concern only people living in this City the votes of district councillors always tip the scales, usually in the wrong direction.

Autumn 2006: Eighty-five can be nothing other than 'old'. When I retired at sixty-two I considered myself a 'late middle-aged' which I could justify by my activities at that time – voluntary work, WEA classes, learning to sail, buying a boat and doing a lot of sailing. By seventy-five I did not mind being called elderly; if I'm here in five years time I shall be 'very old'.

I am not gregarious by nature – I have joined few clubs or societies. I was invited to join Rotary but found it was mainly for the local small businessman. In addition, I lived some miles out of town. I worked in a large organization and did not have much to contribute to the club, though two of my colleagues enjoyed their membership.

When we retired we came south and I immediately became a 'Friend' of the Cathedral and involved myself in a lot of jobs – counting collections, delivering newsletters, serving and so on and my wife did work for the Red Cross. So we have a lot of acquaintances (people whom we invited in for our evening meal occasionally) but we have never made close friends – someone who one could call on and be welcomed at any time.

As we got older and my wife's eyesight became a problem we gave up entertaining. Living in a block of flats, we have neighbours who are very friendly [and] whom we could ask for help at any time, but the majority of the sixteen flats are lived in by people as old as we are. Our major interest is in the lives of our four children (all over forty) and four grandchildren, whom we see only a couple of times a year as we are a family scattered from Cornwall to NQ Scotland. I have given these biographical details to try to explain how I am not equipped to make reliable comments on relationships with other people. I accept people as they are.

Age and ageing was not important till my parents became old, and in the past few years it had been important to us. My wife was a widow when we married and I remember saying to her on our honeymoon that we were going to stay together of the rest of our lives and that then I would [want] her to die first so that she would never be lonely again.

What are the gains and losses of getting older? Until I left the army when I was twenty-five, getting older meant gaining greater knowledge and confidence in oneself. Things levelled out a bit then, though I never stopped learning all my life.

Age became important only because physical strength declined and I was less able to pull my weight in a mixed crew on a larger boat. I feel flattered when people occasionally express surprise that I am as old as eighty-five!

Now lack of confidence in my sense of balance means that I have to take a walking stick when I go out. I always set out with 'head up, chin in, shoulders back and back straight', as our drill sergeant said, but not for very long, if I am on my feet for two hours I feel pretty tired for the rest of the day … Now I have an afternoon nap – only I lie on my bed and listen to a book on tape till I drop off.

We have a number of private homes locally providing various degrees of sheltered accommodation up to full-time nursing homes but often it is not easy to find room in one's first choice. I have visited people in them and they provide varying degrees of luxury. The best are very expensive. I find it very depressing to see old people – almost all women – sitting aimlessly waiting for their lives to end. In a way I'd like their idleness if it wasn't enforced.

I have far more to do than I really want and there are dozens of books I want to read, or reread. I get calls from the cathedral asking if I can fill in for someone who is ill. I have our mail to deal with because of my wife's sight. We have as much as we can [have] delivered including a big order by e-mail for groceries once a month but I still have to go into town for the GPO, the library, the bank, the chemist and so on.

I do things so slowly nowadays too and have to do them twice because I got it wrong the first time. My typing has so many mistakes that even this [Mass Observation] directive becomes a bit of a chore. My wife says it's my own fault because little of it is essential, but I am reluctant to give things up. I decided to stop driving a few months ago, after sixty-six years with a license; I was doing so many stupid things at home, most of which were recoverable, but one mistake on the road and it could be fatal. I am still getting used to it but one can get a lot of taxis from what one saves from having no car.

I have an uncle in a comfortable Masonic home. He is ninety-five [and] has had a stroke which leaves him unable to use his arms properly so [he] can't even turn on his radio unaided. His sight precludes his watching television or reading and he wouldn't be able to operate a cassette recorder to listen to books on tape. Nonetheless, he remains remarkably cheerful when we speak to him on the phone and his memory is better by far than mine. He can remember the names of our children and the lives they lead. I sincerely hope that neither I nor my wife would reach that state of disability.

We have both signed 'living wills' and both agree that a quick death is far preferable to being an invalid, or becoming more and more dependent on other people. Were I to be alone I would be in the fortunate position to be able to afford to pay someone to provide daily help. I don't want to have to leave this flat, particularly as it would leave my children – with varying degrees – worrying about my welfare. I know virtually nothing about 'support services' apart from what one reads in the paper. They are underfunded, the staff are overstretched and I would be very unhappy to have to depend on them.

That there is a need for charities such as *Age Concern* and *Help the Aged* show[s] the extent of the problem. It is a disgrace to all of us that so many old people die in poverty and loneliness. They cannot all have no relations at all so the stigma of neglect falls on their families first. That takes the argument back to what their families saw when they were children – what standards their parents set for them. So we get into single-parent families, deprived childhoods and so on. Society is a web of strands coming from all directions. It is far too complex for legislation and administration to cope with all the detail and we have to return to the individual again.

Our government at the moment is far too concerned with the mess they themselves have got us in to in the Middle East, and with renewing our unnecessary nuclear weapons to be able to devote much time – and still more important – money to the important issues connected with the welfare of the voters.

I hope things will improve so that eventually home care is available at the level required for everyone needing it – and that means finding people willing to earn a living providing it. Which will mean changing many people's attitude to old people; young people are reluctant to face the fact that they too will be old one day so they push the whole situation to the very back of their minds.

I have been very fortunate throughout my life. Now I read the obituaries in the *Guardian* and see that well over half those mentioned are younger than I am. It well might be that this is my last contribution to M-O!

2009, aged 88: I am eighty-eight. I don't know what the odds are but it is not at all unlikely that I shall be dead by this time next year.

I can't do much in the way of exercise – I use a stick about the house and an electric scooter when I go out … My muscles have wasted through lack of use. My weight when I was really fit was 144 lbs. It is now down to 126. I am not grumbling; I have a wonderful GP who keeps an eye on me, as she has since we moved here twenty-five years ago. I find more than enough to do – largely because everything takes so long. Typing something like this means frequently going back to make corrections. Yesterday I had to put a couple of small screws into a hinge on a piece of furniture. A five-minute job for one of my children, half-an-hour for me.

I read the *Guardian* – I can still do the quick crossword – and sometimes write to them. I've been published perhaps half-a-dozen times in the past thirty years or so! I have always got a library book. I love music, but even with hearing aids I cannot appreciate it now – I can see the violinists playing on the TV screen but when they reach a certain pitch I can no longer hear them. I use a lot of e-mails to keep in touch with family, especially grandchildren and a few very old friends – the two most important were with me in Burma.

Before I go to sleep – I sleep very well, except for hourly 'comfort breaks' – I think, 'One night I might not wake up again', and hope that it is as easy as that.

I am very sad to be leaving such a cruel and chaotic world for my grandchildren and their grandchildren. The climate changes that are already inevitable will cause vast upheaval – unimaginable population movements as tides flood whole countries or new deserts cause starvation. I can only hope that my descendants are equipped mentally and physically to cope with whatever they are faced with in a humane and practical way.

I have always been interested in politics but the fact is an election next year seems a minor event to me – whatever happens won't have much effect on what lies ahead for me.

2010, aged 88: In the block of sixteen flats in which I live there are at least three people [aged] over ninety, and I doubt if more than another three are [aged] under eighty, so we live in a restrictive environment. My children recognize our limitations in outlook and I imagine our three teenage grandchildren find it hard to understand our thoughts at all.

I find it sad that the government cannot discriminate between the reasonably well-off pensioner and the desperately poor. I, like many I know, do not need winter fuel allowance for example. It is easy to give it away but not easy to get it to the really hard-up old people.

I find little of interest on television apart from things which remind us of the beauties of nature, with which we used to be in regular contact, and I really don't care how old people are characterized in the media or by government. Ronald Blythe uses his knowledge of Akenfield to reflect on old age in *The View in Winter*, which is a sympathetic and accurate reflection on what it is like to be old. Somewhere on my shelves I have another beautiful book about growing old gracefully by a lovely elder lady but I can't find it. As with so many setbacks nowadays one just has to accept it.

I am eighty-nine next month and mere existence can be quite hard work! Everything takes much longer – from tying shoelaces to brushing one's teeth. Redoing something one has done wrong is also a major time-waster. I feel fit but have a trapped nerve at the base of my spine due to osteoarthritis, which causes a lot of pain down my left leg right to my toes. I have tried numerous painkillers, but their side-effects end up by being as unpleasant as their original purpose.

I only have one regular commitment. Every Tuesday morning I do a one-hour duty at the Cathedral greeting visitors. We are known as 'Doorkeepers', and there are well over 100 of us working in pairs through an eight-hour day in summer and six hours in winter. With a walking stick I can just about manage one hour on my feet. It is very interesting to meet people from all over the world and in many cases be able to offer them a leaflet in their own language which describes what they see as they go round the wonderful building.

We go to Matins on most Sundays – weather permitting. A big disadvantage of my lameness is that we cannot walk anywhere together – my wife goes ahead and I catch her up by the time she has arrived. I am no longer a Christian, though I was for the greater part of my life. Time to reflect since I retired has led to my becoming a Deist – I recognize that there is an omniscient Creator but we are in no position to go any further – trying to describe it leads to argument and ultimately conflict. However I like the music and the atmosphere and find it easy to sit and contemplate while the service goes on. The sermons usually give one something to think about too.

Another irregular commitment I do is street collections. I have done them for years and nowadays I can do them whilst sitting down on my scooter. I still do the RNLI, the Wildlife Trust, Stonepillow (which started by providing overnight shelter for people sleeping on the streets but has now spread its objectives) and the Hospice. I am fascinated by people's reactions to the sight of a collecting box ahead of them!

My wife and I have separate rooms because we have different sleeping patterns. I used to take her breakfast in bed, but I am unsafe carrying a tray now so she gets it herself and takes it back to bed. Having had many months in hospitals, I hate eating in bed, so around 8 a.m. I put on my dressing gown and have my cereal and toast from a tray I prepared before I went to bed. I do half the quick crossword – leaving half for my wife – and look at the Sports pages. The rest of the *Guardian* is by my chair to fill in the rest of the day.

After a shower I am usually ready for the day about ten o'clock. I look to see if there are any e-mails. We have a small top-floor flat and though we have interesting views it can feel restrictive if one is here for days without going out. My wife buys online for her major needs but doing the odd shopping is easy for me by scooter.

I always say I will not lie down after lunch but the need becomes overwhelming and it is a wonderful relief to relax, flat on one's back, to take the load off one's legs for half-an-hour plus. I almost always drop off to sleep. I sleep quite well at night – with three or four bladder awakenings – so in all I spend a good eight hours of my twenty-four asleep, even though I have rarely done anything tiring during the day.

I had twenty-three years with the [international manufacturing] company and have now been a pensioner for twenty-eight. I have been very lucky.

2011, aged 90: Ageing and care is something very much in our minds. I am ninety and my wife is eighty-six. We live in a comfortable flat and hope we shall not have to leave it. My wife was an SRN Sister so is an excellent carer and fortunately is well enough to look after me. Her health has been dogged with eye problems but they have stabilized and she can read large print books. Unfortunately I am now suffering from osteoarthritis, which is giving me increasing difficulty with pain and restricted mobility.

We have paid domestic help on two mornings a week. Our neighbours in the other flats are elderly too so we can expect help from them only in an emergency. If one of us needed full-time help – me becoming bedridden for example – we have enough savings to pay for it for four years or so, but we would be reluctant to have to use what we have always regarded as a legacy for our children. As a very last resort, we have the flat on a very long lease – the sale of which would provide for as long as either of us could conceivably need.

Our disabled daughter – she has a car and is reasonably mobile – can get to us in about two hours, but she has a husband and we could not expect her to spend a long period with us. Our elder daughter is divorced and is bringing up three teenage children whilst studying for a Ph.D., so we would not expect her to have time to help. Our elder boy lives in northwest Scotland, and is a director of a largish business in Inverness. His wife is self-employed and has a lot of business travelling. Our younger boy, who has been a difficult rolling stone all his life, is a self-employed farm worker and has established himself as a knowledgeable vineyard manager. He would be free to provide live-in help in the home if we needed it, but [this] would not be our first choice.

My parents both needed care at the end of their lives. My father had surgery for a bowel problem. He was a little over eighty. He spent time in hospital after surgery but the doctor said his mind would never recover from the effect of the anaesthetic. He eventually was sent home but was more than my mother could handle – she was four years older than he – as he was incontinent as well as confused. The doctor arranged for him to go to a nursing home and got a charity associated with the business my father had been in [to] contribute to the fees. My sister and I paid the small balance.

It [the nursing home] had some twenty-plus residents. I had no experience of such places and only realized later that its standards were very low. My father was not happy there and desperately wanted to return to his wife. One very cold December afternoon he left the house in carpet slippers and a dressing gown over his pyjamas and walked a good mile along an icy main road before a police car on patrol spotted him and took him back. How he avoided pneumonia I will never understand.

He shared space on a landing as his 'bedroom'. One night he got out of bed and had a fall. He died before I heard what had happened. It so happened that a cousin of mine in the Police was the Coroner's Officer. He realized that there should be an inquest, but he equally knew my father since boyhood and knew full well that the last thing he would want would be to 'make a fuss'. We felt embarrassed too as our doctor had arranged for Dad to go into the home and he would have been involved at any inquest. We decided to do nothing. That was some thirty years ago – I hope there are no care homes like that now but unfortunately it still seems possible.

I hope that NHS hospitals have higher standards but it all depends on available money. If a Hospital Trust has to cut back on staffing costs and there are insufficient nurses to provide the very demanding needs of the old people in their charge something is going to get overlooked.

Trace all that back to the Chancellor of the Exchequer as the individual who allotted insufficient money to Health and go one step further back and you find that we, the taxpayer are responsible because we complain at the amount of tax we are already paying and would vote against any increase.

My mother was living alone [before she went into care]. I worked 300 miles away and it was impossible to get down to her for more than one weekend a month. If work gave me a reason for going to London I would make an opportunity to go down with my mother – fifty miles away – for the night. However I wrote her a card and sent it with a small packet of sweets every day. My sister lived in London and could go for the day once a week or so.

My mother had a very good home helper at one time, who had retired. She [the home helper] was pleased to respond to a plea from my sister to keep a close eye on our mother. We paid her what she requested and explained to our mother that Mrs Atkins would come back to help as she used to. My mother said she would pay the hourly rate she had previously – not realizing that wages had inflated significantly since Mrs. Atkins had been with her before. We ensured that Mrs. Atkins accepted this and we made up the difference, unbeknown to our mother.

Eventually our mother became too unreliable to live alone and the local authority arranged for her to go to a care home. When I was a child it had been known as 'the workhouse': a large Victorian building accepting the nightly arrival of the tramps who were making their way along the coast. It may have had permanent residents as well, but I was not old enough to be interested. The atmosphere was friendly – the inmates were all in bed, but I think most of them were able to get up and walk. When we visited there was a wheelchair in which we took her for a walk in the country lanes, which we had all known years before when as a family we used to go for Sunday walks.

My mother was not happy – [it was] no fault of the home, but she 'wanted to go back to her little house' and was unable to understand why not. Fortunately she was there for less than a year.

I hope I will die quickly with the minimum of fuss for all concerned. I can imagine circumstances where illness left me with such pain and hopelessness that euthanasia would seem the best solution. I hope not, as I know it would be bound to cause unhappiness in the family. It is certainly something that should be readily available for anyone choosing it, and that means people should not have to travel abroad to access it. It becomes so much more expensive that many people cannot afford it. People who are against it should not have to rely on such handicaps to support their cause.

I have bought a lovely grave plot in a Natural Burial Ground surrounded with beautiful views of the Downs. I have arranged for a bamboo coffin – for years after the war I worked in the Burma teak forests and my home was always made of bamboo. I shall feel at home. Thus I have contributed to the environment by avoiding cremation, which uses a lot of either electricity or gas.

The Government has the difficult task of demonstrating to people that the care which they will need in old age is going to be very expensive and they will have to begin to pay for it now. Taxation in various forms must raise money for this. It might be a good idea to keep money raised for pensions quite separate from other taxes so that people can see what is being put aside for their future.

A great debate is needed as to what we should provide for people too old to work. First of all we must realize that our working lives will get longer as people get older, unless we are prepared to pay very heavy taxation now to fund it. Retirement age should be the decision of the individual, with pension benefits calculated accordingly. Things could be simplified if all the benefit[s] were in monthly pension form. If the pension is adequate why should there be a need to be 'add-ons'? Free prescriptions, TV Licenses, fuel allowances etc. should be abolished. The administrative savings would be significant, and people ought to make their own decisions about spending their pension.

If a pensioner can no longer live without help from a relative or carer the State – perhaps best through the Local Authority – has to become involved. To what level is debatable: kindness and comfort, but not luxury, and keeping people in their own homes where possible. Taking people into a care home is the last resort as such places cannot avoid being seen as the place where people go to die. The quality of staff is most important and suitable people, who must be devoted carers, will not be easy to find. Good training ending in a 'Qualified Carer' certificate and a good salary should follow.

Over the time-span involved, people ought to be able to get used to the idea of care for their parents as being part of family life. I have lived for some time in India, and elderly parents appear as a matter of course within the close family circle of the friends made.

3

'To Me, Life and Work Are Linked'

Margaret Christopher

Margaret Christopher *was born in 1927 and grew up in rural Wales as an only child with a governess. She is now divorced and lives in a granny flat below her daughter's family home in London, in what she describes as an ideal arrangement. Margaret's employment has included part-time administrative duties for a charity, bereavement counselling, and full-time and voluntary work for a busy Citizen's Advice Bureau. She has also been closely involved with the local West Indian community. Her ex-husband was a 'failed experimental novelist', and she reflects poignantly on their relationship breakdown. She spent much of her life feeling like a 'perpetual outsider' and regrets never marrying a successful writer or academic and thereby gaining entry to a liberal intellectual circle. Margaret finds it 'delightfully peaceful' to be single, however, and is glad to escape the 'stigma' of spinsterhood due to her divorced status.*

Margaret feels relatively fit and healthy, having recovered from a breast cancer scare. Working voluntarily well into old age gives her purpose. She hates being idle and likes to stay busy with constant tasks. Margaret writes in detail about the aged population, the healthcare system and poor government provisions for aged care: 'Everyone is, or can be, aware of old age and its problems in a manner that did not exist for my grandparents and much less than now even for my parents.' Margaret professes that she 'coped shamefully badly' with the physical and mental deterioration of her elderly mother and 'best loved spinster aunt'. She felt unprepared and ignorant as to how she might assist. Margaret finds it hard to relate to younger generations, which puts a strain on her relationship with her granddaughters: 'We are all really,

really fond of one another, but it's definitely "them and me": even the cats feel this!' She has strong views on immigrants, asylum seekers and race relations and is highly critical towards sensationalizing media. She is an atheist and a supporter of euthanasia.

Aside from the three main directives discussed in the introduction and appendix of this book, the material in this chapter is also taken from replies to the following MO directives: 1992; 'The Pace of Life', 1994 'Death and Bereavement', 1998 'Staying Well and Everyday Life', 2000 'Gays and the Family', and 2011 'Ageing and Care'.

Winter 1992, aged 65: As I write, I am two months short of my sixty-sixth birthday and in May I must retire from my full-time job because of my age. This annoys me very much, especially as 1993 is supposed to be 'The European Year of the Elderly'. I enjoy working, feel capable of continuing in my job for at least another couple of years and dread the unstructured days which threaten to lie ahead.

Sometimes when I look at myself in the mirror I am frankly appalled at the sight I see with its flabby neck, grey hair and undeniably elderly expression: this in spite of people telling me I look younger than my age – and meaning it. I sometimes jokingly refer to myself as old, and must indeed seem so to my grandchildren; but I have decided to my own satisfaction that old age starts, undeniably, at seventy-five. I think there is truth in the expression 'You're as old as you feel' and physically I barely feel old at all, with very few aches or pains and a capacity to work hard and to go on long walks. But some of my friends, even ones a few years younger, are much less active than I because of their various ailments, most commonly arthritis, or their creeping lethargy.

So physically I scarcely feel elderly (except that when climbing hills in a group I tend to be the last – but then I was never very good on hills). But mentally I have fallen into a trap which I always hoped I would avoid but which I now see as inevitable: without doubt the world in all its aspects is growing steadily worse, particularly in terms of manners, morals, greed, attitudes to life and to work and obligations, while the word 'duty' is never heard. I notice this at work where most of my colleagues, who are aged around forty, seem to have little or no sense of the obligations with which I was brought up; and I cannot help feeling this is a kind of impoverishment. This leads to a rather stuffy, disapproving attitude on my part, even though I realize how much the world has changed in terms of consumerism and lifestyles, with parents indulging their children but demanding very little in terms of reciprocal obligation (e.g. thanks for, or even appreciation of presents).

My daughter had her fortieth birthday in 1992 and it seemed to cause her real anguish as she clearly saw it as some sort of turning point. I think I have taken the start of all my decades (excepting my fiftieth) fairly philosophically in the realization that since they are inevitable one just has to turn them to the best advantage possible. But when I reach seventy in four years time that really may be a turning point – it all depends on what I am doing at the time and how involved I feel.

I do not believe in reincarnation or any form of afterlife but am convinced that this is our one chance and therefore we should make the greatest possible use of it. I feel passionate about not wasting a moment of my remaining life but putting every minute of every day to some good use; and I think that, coincidentally, this helps me remain active – I just haven't got time to be ill.

I am not very sure whether ageing affects men and women differently, but I tend to think it's not their sex but their circumstances and attitudes which determine the way in which, or speed at which, they age. In the past – though rather less so today – most of the world's leading public figures have been old men, and of course one always used to be told (and to believe) that wisdom increased with age. Now, sadly, I have to admit to not being noticeably wiser than my forty-year-old daughter, and my elderly friends tend to be prejudiced rather than wise.

Perhaps the lack of accumulated wisdom is due to my own character (I think it is), or perhaps I expect too much of the concept of wisdom: I am always looking for it and not finding it. My husband, whom I left when he was sixty-four, showed all the symptoms of ageing in a particularly un-self-aware way, and I believe this has continued, whereas I myself believe one has to watch oneself ever more closely to prevent oneself becoming either boring or out of touch. I think I am more aware of nuances of behaviour than I used to be and occasionally I feel others may be influenced, however reluctantly, by my own attitudes – although I try not to flaunt them.

From the vantage point of sixty-five, the losses which come with growing older far outweigh the gains, even when one is well and comparatively strong. There is the constant realization that one's life is finite, that one may not be here in ten years, most likely will not be in twenty years and certainly not in thirty years. And that means never knowing about future generations of one's family or even what will happen to the beloved daughter.

One does tire more quickly, though that doesn't matter if one lives alone and can rest; can eat much less and therefore has to be watchful all the time to resist food temptations. I tend to fall asleep at odd times, particularly at meetings however hard I fight against it – and this can be very embarrassing. Attention to detail slips in a particularly annoying way and concentration flags more easily. I find it much harder to be interested in casual conversation and, to my annoyance find it extremely difficult to talk to teenagers or people in their early twenties because their whole life experience is so different.

I seem to spend far too much time saying 'where have I put my glasses?' to myself or anyone who happens to be listening, and without them I can read nothing except really big letters. Then there is the fear of 'becoming gaga' with all its boringness for others and humiliation for oneself; or of becoming physically ill or breaking bones.

These days, the advantages to counterbalance this catalogue of woes, present and future, are not very many. But top of the list from the practical point of view are travel concessions, followed by reduced theatre, cinema and exhibition prices. In London, us lucky pensioners can travel completely free on buses and the underground and this gives us a huge incentive to explore to the very limits of the city.

This leads me on to describe how I shall spend my remaining years: seeing new places and catching up on books, pictures and music for which until now I have not had nearly enough time. I find the thought of the University of the Third Age rather depressing and don't envisage joining it; but I shall read widely in history, particularly that of the Middle East. I shall travel as much as I can afford and explore more of England by bicycle in the summers. I shall garden, sew, mend my clothes, try to cook more interestingly, help my daughter with the children, type authors' manuscripts if they come my way, go for long country walks, keep up with my friends, do some voluntary work and generally keep busy. I shall also try and make sense of my life and failed marriage by writing an account of both.

My immediate experiences [of the care of older people] were two-fold and began with my best loved spinster aunt, a retired civil servant who also developed Alzheimer's in her eighties. An older cousin of mine was in the frontline and found our aunt a place in a home where I think they were kind to her and she was allowed to have a cat. I suffered deeply over the disintegration of this grande dame, who gradually became anxious and helpless, wandering, understanding nothing and repeating herself endlessly. Now I know this is commonplace, but no one at that time had prepared me for it.

This overlapped with my mother, and as an only child with an unhelpful husband I coped shamefully badly. She too was in her eighties, lived alone, had a fall and was taken to hospital where she spent the last months of her life. The whole period of her old age and my behaviour towards her at that time now constitutes a deep and desperate shame on my part for my insensitivity to her needs from when she fell on a station platform and broke her pelvis, later had two toes amputated, became incontinent and suffered from angina, while rarely complaining.

She lived in Oxford; I lived in London but was often abroad with my husband and the help I gave her was minimal. The only reason why I wish I could believe in an afterlife is so that I could ask her forgiveness. I think she loved me very much, but I never appreciated her as I should and we never understood one another. I see now, very clearly, all the things I should have done, but at the same time some part of my neglect was due to plain ignorance of what was needed.

Since that time, which ended on Christmas Day in 1969, [...] I have thought much more about the acute problems of old age. At this moment we have in the family an eighty-eight-year-old cousin who has suffered several small strokes and is still living at home with vastly expensive live-in care. I spent this Christmas with her and found the experience deeply depressing as she is beyond conversation, the strokes having had the effect of garbling her speech, and it is hard to tell how much she understands. A life of that kind does seem to me pointless.

My father died suddenly in his armchair aged seventy-two, after years of winter misery from bronchitis, but still working. I think he knew it was the only solution as his chest and his sciatica were not going to improve and I find it hard to understand why people cling to a life which has nothing left to offer. I only hope I shall know when it is time for me to go – and go.

As I wrote above in relation to my own experience, I don't think that most of us respect old people as we were taught to do; but it is difficult if not impossible to do so while watching their personalities disintegrate. I have seen in the last few years clever men turn into bumbling incontinents and have been left feeling that it must be purest agony for a wife in these circumstances to watch somebody she loved and respected become simply a zombie because his body has outlived his mind – or equally, of course, but rarer, a husband looking after his wife in a similar state.

It is an enormous strain for a husband, a wife, a son or daughter to have charge of a dementing old person and not entirely surprising when something snaps. Some of the most distressing sights I have ever seen have been the day rooms of the geriatric hospitals where the old people sit in rows around the walls, looking completely vacant as they sleep or mumble, the television perpetually on, but perpetually miscomprehended. To attempt to keep some spark of awareness alive in them would be labour intensive and time consuming, but without individual contact they lose all dignity and even, it sometimes seems, their very human qualities.

As a spin-off from my regular work, I am committee secretary of a club, now in its twelfth year, for West Indian pensioners, which is run as a day centre providing lunch and excellent facilities for handicrafts, which they love to do. Sometimes we bring in dementing old people, but the problem is their tendency to wander out and get lost. Our staff are very patient, but their wages are extremely low and this reflects the commitment of the government to provide the kind of second rather than first class service old people need and deserve. To keep our driver, who is exceptionally committed and conscientious, we have to supplement his official wage from our meagre charitable funds; and for the same reason of low pay scales we have had huge difficulty in appointing an overall administrator with the necessary skills. After vicissitudes, I think our club is now a model of its kind for we keep a close eye on our old people, visit them in hospital, see their benefits are correct, cook fresh food for them daily, respect their diets and deliver meals to the housebound [...]

In our borough there is quite good provision of sheltered housing for the elderly and some of the houses have excellent wardens, on whom in the circumstances much depends. There is a new geriatric unit in our local hospital and there are two sheltered houses specifically for elderly Afro-Caribbeans; but there are still a lot of old people living alone and dependent upon a rather inadequate service which seems to be the weakest link in the chain in spite of its vital importance. Some home helps skimp their work, a few are dishonest and the regulations do not seem to allow them enough time to see to housework as opposed to shopping. It seems to me that their quality is low because their pay is low and in my observation the office staff who organize them are poorly trained and motivated.

If I were old and housebound, rather than continue to live in a basement with no outlook, as I do at the moment, I think I would prefer to have a room in a sheltered house with sunshine coming in at the window and a garden outside. But then again the rooms in these 'custom built' blocks tend to be very small and it would be almost an impossible wrench to part with nearly all my books and bibelots. So I can only hope that by the time I reach this stage we shall have moved house and I may be able to continue to be with my daughter and behave sufficiently well for her to be able to cope with me. I do dread hospitals and doctors for they seem to expect elderly patients to take quite a horrifying number of different pills in spite of their vagueness about remembering to do so. I strongly believe in euthanasia and I intend to write a 'living will' to set out instructions that I should not be kept alive after a stroke. I hope to die with dignity and in control of my faculties.

I don't think priority should be given to care of the elderly over that for the handicapped, the mentally ill and the other categories of vulnerable people of all ages: I just think that if we regard ourselves as humane and responsible instead of greedy and selfish (in which direction we appear to have been going over the last twelve years), we should be prepared to be taxed enough to maintain a proper level of services for everyone in need. And I think we should carry this message to the politicians.

Spring 1992, aged 65: I am: female, divorced after 30 married years, aged 65 and still at work as an 'administrative officer' in a London Citizens Advice Bureau. I live in a granny flat with my daughter, her partner and two children occupying the house over my head. The children are 9 and 4 years old. My daughter is a freelance editor, working at home. Her partner is a self-employed designer and maker of furniture, with a workshop but no employees – at present suffering from the recession.

When I was a child, growing up in the country, life seemed to move very slowly and very tediously. It felt as if nothing exciting was ever going to happen to me – just waiting, waiting. Between the ages of twenty-two and fifty-three – my married life – it continued to be slow and tedious for long stretches of time, especially living in hot southern European countries for periods of two or three months in rented houses away from friends, books, entertainments and the comforts of home.

This of course made me tremendously conscious of time, a consciousness which also increases with age. From [the age of] fifty-three to sixty-five (the present), time has been wonderfully agreeable and I never feel that soul-searing tedium which has had the lasting effect of making me aware of every day and almost every hour. I am still working – officially a thirty-seven hour week, but I usually do several hours in addition since I firmly believe that life and work are indivisible, and if work is useful and enjoyable there is no hardship in carrying on with it beyond statutory hours. I notice that younger colleagues veer, if anything, in the opposite direction, skimping over their hours, and I do realize that those of us who have jobs we enjoy are a lucky minority.

When I really fall to pieces, feel tired and fed up is when I don't have enough to do; so I have learned to plan my life so there is always slightly too much. For example, when I come home from work I type author's manuscripts and students' theses (irregularly), and am never happier than when typing away until eleven or twelve [o'clock] at night. Or I write letter, a diary, these directives, and I garden for as many hours a week as I can spare. I cook for myself every day, watch a certain amount of television (plays and documentaries) sew and mend, and of course read. So the only time in the twenty-four hours when I am doing nothing is before I fall asleep at night, or sometimes when I am talking to my daughter in the house upstairs.

I realized I carry this obsession with using every minute too far, for I resent playing with my grandchildren or taking them out on their bicycles, when I could be doing all the things I have lined up for myself. In vain do I tell myself it's just as important to be playing with them. That's the corollary of the already mentioned feeling that life and work are one: the danger is that the work element comes to dominate and playing or being idle becomes equivalent to wasting time.

When I began to answer this directive I was under notice of retirement because of my age and this threw me into a complete state of panic. The thought of waking to an empty, unstructured day in a small dark flat [has] now receded, at least until 1993, and I realize that if I think carefully there are very many things I can do to fill the gap left by work: principally studying or doing voluntary work, or a combination of both – with one whole summer of forays by bus and bicycle into parts of the country I know little of. I must also train myself to spend more time sitting and reading. Sitting and letting one's mind wander is another matter: to contemplate the past brings distress at all which had been lost through 'progress', while to look into the future fills one with gloom at the world's growing problems. I can think about the present while cooking, bathing or doing other chores.

What suffers from this quite busy life is reading, writing, looking and the finer points of gardening, but I tell myself there will be plenty of time for these when I do have to retire.

A lot of this serenity is due to luck in having a job I like, no stress from long daily journeys and no worries about money or housing.

If I were to think of myself as an object it would be a steadily ticking clock, calm and measured for the most part, continuing in the same way until the mechanism, becomes worn – but with occasional oilings and windings (i.e. treats and rethinks) until it finally grinds to a halt in death.

There is nothing to beat the belief that there is no such thing as the after-life to make one determined to make the best possible use of the only life we have: every minute of every year counts. To my mind, among the losers are those who endure the present in the hope of a better death in 'the life to come'.

Spring 1994, aged 67: I suppose one could say I was obsessed with death from early adolescence. I still have three large scrapbooks specially ordered from Harrods into which I used to paste obituaries cut from *The Times*.

Now I am sixty-seven and death seems much more real, although by no means imminent! I take a great deal of comfort from knowing that when I am dead I shall lie in my oak coffin in a Welsh country graveyard, which is like a wild flower meadow in spring and early summer and is separated only by a wall from fields of sheep and cattle, with no more than a couple of farmhouses in sight.

I visit this churchyard every year. I have the right to be buried there because it is where I was christened: I say this because I now have no religious belief or thoughts of an afterlife. Christianity itself and its doctrines of resurrection, heaven and hell seem to me to be patently man-made ways of trying to get round the actual futility and meaninglessness of life. This might sound bleak, but I hope it is intellectually honest: man's great sin is that of pride, in thinking that we matter and are specially privileged in the universe, whereas it is we who perpetrate what looks as though it may be its eventual destruction by our greed.

Apart from assuring my burial place and making a will, I have not made any preparations for death, but I plan to do so. I am very afraid of paralysis and being unable to move or speak yet still remaining alive; but I am not afraid of death itself and may even welcome it. I am rather afraid of sinking into the depression which some old people suffer, and I have a good supply of pills to take if I want to end my life. I most certainly believe in euthanasia under certain circumstances and with appropriate safeguards and shall try to ensure I am not kept alive in a vegetable state: that seems to be a refined form of cruelty.

During the 1970s I lost my mother, my favourite aunt, a great friend who I had been looking after, another much-loved friend and several other people of whom I was fond. In no case was I there at the moment of death and this I very deeply regret. I feel I let them down by not being there and this remains an unhealed wound in the background of my life. As a result of all these deaths – and galvanized by my own separation (another form of bereavement) – I became a bereavement counsellor in the 1980s and continued with this in my spare time for six years. During that period I sometimes felt I was suffocating under a tide of other people's grief, and finally I stopped. I emerged a harder, not a better person, which is not to say that I didn't have some marked successes with my clients as well as some failures. What made me harder were the insights into people's self-delusion, which I found deeply depressing.

Autumn 1998, aged 71: I am employed part-time (twenty hours a week) [at the Citizens Advice Bureau] after having retired from my previous occupation because of my age. I am extremely well, much fitter than some younger friends and many contemporaries in spite of never doing yoga, exercises or swimming. I walk, cycle to work and garden. I attribute this good health partly to coming from 'sound stock' – my mother never was sick nor had a headache in her life. I was sickly as a child, but since growing up I have had no serious illnesses except for a breast cancer episode in 1990, which was diagnosed and treated rapidly and successfully. I take no medication except calcium pills started recently.

I feel that both diet and frame of mind have a great deal to do with good health. I eat no processed, tinned or packaged food, butter not margarine, full fat mild and fresh meat, poultry or fish; vegetables, but little salad and no fruit except orange juice with my nightly whiskey. I drink 'real' coffee, wine, spirits, bottled water and elder-flower cordial – quite a narrow range of foods and seldom organic because of the expense. Although seriously dismayed about a number or aspects of modern life, because I can choose how to conduct my own I enjoy my days and my work and I feel this must have a bearing on my good health. The days are often long and encompass voluntary work as well.

Approaching [the age of] seventy-two, I am of course very well aware that parts of me will begin to experience the effects of wear and tear, though scans following the broken ankle showed my bones to be in good order at present.

Sometimes I feel panicky and depressed at the certain knowledge that in the end decline will be inevitable; but most of the time I am too busy to dwell on it for long and the sensible way is to make the most of the present. Last week I proved I can still walk fifteen miles in a day without feeling more than just reasonably tired. Life is too short for any of it to be wasted by feeling ill!

Autumn 2000, aged 73: I love my grand-daughters, but there is much about their upbringing of which I disapprove. When we settled down together [in a shared house] I took a conscious decision, and having seen how an interfering older person can undermine relationships, I think I was right in deciding that one either keeps completely quiet – hard though it may be not to criticize – or one could end by destroying affection forever.

So I think it deplorable that the girls have apparently never been taught to shake hands or make polite conversation, open doors or help old ladies with their shopping, let alone take part in any community activities. I wish they would talk to me about their lives. But then I realize that if they trust and confide in their mother, as they do, a grandmother is not really necessary. Her role can be vital when parents fail, but [it] is redundant if they succeed. And, because I somehow contrive to be modern in some ways but deliberately old-fashioned in others – with 'values' and lifestyle pared down to the basics and no wish to be on the internet, rent videos or have a mobile phone – I almost live in a different world to theirs: a world in which they are not interested. All things considered, it's lucky we get on as well as we do.

Finally, as to family occasions: weddings, funerals or significant birthdays. I always used to look forward to them, as I did to Christmas, but was usually disappointed. Either most of the family were not interested in me, [and] we had nothing in common, or they were even perhaps actively disapproving; or more recently there is a generation gap. I am now separated from the younger family members by two generations and have very little idea of how to talk to the teens and twenties despite living with two of them. So I sit in a corner with, if possible, other 'oldies', and watch. I do so wish I was more flexible, but one is stuck with one's nature however hard one tries.

Summer 2002, aged 75: This year I was seventy-five years old in March; but as I am still working a little, the first part of the day went to writing up minutes I had taken at a meeting the morning before. Then I went to Sotheby's in Bond Street to look at two nineteenth-century portraits of sisters who must have been my great, great, aunts and were now the property of strangers and about to be sold. Afterwards, a fruitless search for a pair of trousers was tiring, so I came home and spent some time working at a tapestry which I am doing for demonstration purposes for a designer of kits. In the evening I dined at a fish restaurant with my daughter, her ex-partner, two grand-daughters, two friends and our lodger. The grandchildren, aged eighteen and fourteen were in bad moods, which somewhat upset me, and they left for home early. The lodger, daughter of a school friend of mine, was somewhat out of her depth. When I reached home I found I had lost a treasured earring which was never seen again.

So altogether, it was not a brilliant day. I wrote in my diary:

It's good to be able to say that I'm still working at seventy-five, and completely well except that my feet hurt. The main consolation for being old, after the family, is the feeling that with friends we have the solidarity of all being in the same precarious position about life and death. I shall die having not read so many books, or done so many things.

The fact that now a birthday is a milestone on the way to the grave is extremely uncomfortable – not much discussed, but all too present in my mind. Many people of my age are decrepit, but I am still vigorous, capable of walking fourteen miles and have to keep on reminding myself that one day I shall have to depend on others.

My daughter and several of her friends have reached fifty this year, and they seem to take it more dolefully than I did, and more apprehensively. This may be because of the increasingly dangerous state of the world, which leads to thoughts of what it will be like in another quarter century. So many changes in the previous twenty-five years seem to have destroyed most of the security one used to be able to feel; added to which the media draw so much attention to ageing and its implications.

Autumn 2003, aged 76: In the last few years in London I have been mugged twice and assaulted once. The assault was in one of those large communal gardens which are hidden behind the houses in this part of London. The first mugging was on my doorstep. The second was in the street as I approached my house, and that actually has shaken me and made me much more aware of the dangers lurking in the streets and parks. So now I stop and look around to see if I am being followed; take only the amount of money I am likely to need and often keep it in my pockets to avoid carrying a handbag. And since all three of my muggers/attackers were black, I can't stop myself from being much more suspicious of black men than I was before these events happened. In other words, urban public spaces have come to be thought of as potential danger zones and in me, vigilance has taken the place of nonchalance.

People tell me sometimes that I am foolish to go walking alone; but to give up doing so would be to constrict my 'freedom' (much abused word, thanks to G. W. Bush), and I think the risks are worth taking.

I mostly meet people completely different from myself. An example of this is during the part-time work I do, involving taking minutes at meetings connected with a branch of the NHS and typing them up in an open plan office. At seventy-six I'm old enough to be the grandmother of almost all the people I meet in this situation; and the mother of the others. Added to which my voice, especially on the telephone, is unmistakeably upper class. This often makes me feel uncomfortable, but they are always polite, even kind, to me and I find it very touching. But inside I feel nervous, and very conscious of my age. An easier aspect of the same job is meeting groups of refugees and asylum seekers who usually don't speak English – and learning through an interpreter what are their thoughts about various aspects of their lives here. They too are touchingly grateful to be talked to in a considerate way, and are very friendly.

Autumn 2006, aged 79: As I shall be eighty-years-old in less than three months time, that leaves no doubt about my position in the scale of age. I have very firm ideas about the categories and the need for people to be aware into which one they fit. For example, it incenses me when both men and women (but men more often) advertise themselves as 'young sixty', or even 'young seventy': it's a mixture of pathetic and ridiculous. I think middle age begins at forty-five, and old age these days at seventy, because life expectation has increased to make a ninetieth birthday seem quite commonplace. It's a most extraordinary contrast with what I remember from my youth of old ladies who acted and dressed as though they really were ancient and decrepit things, to be treated with the greatest respect and rather terrifying to the young.

Of course I have 'changed over the years in how I think about age and aging', and I have always been very conscious of the need to make the most of life. The crunch point for me came when I was fifty-three, living in circumstances which I knew I could not endure for the rest of my life. By the kindness of fate I was offered a job, which meant leaving husband and home and beginning a new, single life which, in spite of the pain and suffering both caused and experienced I have never regretted because it gave me twenty years of work, and even today continued work as a volunteer. To me, life and work are linked – eighty which I know is easy to say only if one has enjoyable work and a pension at the end of it.

I think men and women tend to age differently, and men often become more entrenched in their thought patterns and habits, while women remain more flexible and open to new ideas. In terms of sexuality, women are glad enough to withdraw from love-making (I refuse to write of 'having sex'), while men all too often in my experience make fools of themselves through unwanted advances within or outside marriage. Of course, there are happily married couples at eighty, but not very many.

After the age of seventy-five I don't think there are any advantages at all in getting older, and plenty of losses which increase year by year. At seventy-eight I found I was so stiff I couldn't get off my bicycle and had to give it away, which was a defining moment. It's not only aches and pains and stiffness, heart problems, deafness and so on; it's the awareness that in many ways old people are a bore. Our mindsets and thought patterns are so different and so increasingly incompatible with the young who are often too impatient to explain computers, iPods, mobile phones and all the possibilities of the internet. I'm typing this on my computer, but I long for my typewriter and some carbon paper! I don't want to buy my clothes, food and holidays online; I would rather visit shops and travel agents.

I think my situation now is ideal. It took shape twenty years ago when my daughter and her then partner wanted to buy a house but had a shortage of money. So they asked me to sell my flat and join with them, but in a self-contained basement. After ten years they parted, so the house was sold and profits divided. My daughter found a house which she and I could afford, and ten years later it is proving the perfect way for me to spend my last years. As long as I remain active and independent I am no liability, but actually an asset in terms of sharing the expenses that go with owning a house. If I become infirm, my two rooms are on one level and very convenient. And I'm never lonely, as so many old people are.

In practical terms, local councils and the Red Cross, Help the Aged and Age Concern are very helpful in providing aids and advice. I expect I shall need a stairlift and a walk-in bath at some point, but I will have to pay for these myself. But a wheelchair, a Zimmer frame and various gadgets will be given to me for free.

I think care in the future should be as it is now at its best, i.e. comprehensive and thoughtful – the only threats to maintenance and the improvement of standards are budgetary cuts and the extraordinary ideas the present government seems to have about the organization of the NHS. Politicians, for one reason or another, are symptomatic of society as a whole in that they don't seem to really care enough to think through policies and their implications in detail and analyse their likely consequences. The result is that innovations don't work and then a whole new batch of 'initiatives' is announced.

As we are often told, people are living longer, which means a higher percentage of elderly. I'm bound to say, it's often difficult to respect them when they are confused or 'gaga'; what is needed is endless patience. Respect as a concept seems to have turned into something of a cliché with a much broader meaning: to be respected, one needs to be deserving of respect. The experience and possible wisdom of the elderly is, I think, less respected than in the past; but that's because the world has changed so much in our lifetime, making many of our experiences irrelevant. The younger generation don't ask my opinions very often and if I offer advice it's very far from certain they will take it!

There is no denying that the cost to the state of providing care for the growing number of elderly is a serious problem – in the light of which it's very hard to understand the private pension debacle engineered by Gordon Brown. Why did he let it happen, and why didn't he correct it? Looking at extreme old age from its threshold, I think it's one of the great conundrums of our time and I'm strongly in favour of voluntary euthanasia, with safeguards from exploitation. So many very old, bedridden, doubly incontinent men and women would be glad to die.

Winter 2009, aged 82: I can't imagine a life without books; I've just counted and found I own seven hundred. Many are kept in my bedroom and I love to lie in bed and gaze at those shelved behind my desk, among them still some waiting to be read.

I talk about books with my daughter sometimes, although her tastes are often different; she loves Swedish thriller writers and some American novelists. Almost all of my friends are dead, so most of my thoughts about what I read stay in my head. This is a great loss, an impoverishment, one of the penalties of old age. If I had more time I think I might join a book group, but it's very unlikely I would fit in with the members, given my age. I don't go to public readings because the pace is too fast; to take in something worthwhile one often needs to read passages more than once to fully grasp their content. I would love to be at the Hay festival, but have never managed it. Some of the authors (on the circuit that year!) attend the Charleston Festival in Sussex, where I choose five discussions each year and find them hugely enjoyable. Sometimes my opinion of the participants is changed one way or other, almost certainly for the better. This year I especially remember the Duchess of Devonshire and Adam Nicholson who were a perfect combination, and I liked Margaret Drabble more after hearing her speak.

In all manner of ways the world seems to have changed with astonishing speed in the last twenty years, and that applies to books and their contents as much as anything else. I find it rather hard to understand the meaning behind the question 'Have representations of your own age group in books seemed true to you?' My age group is as diverse as any other; I don't suppose many old people read sociological books about our age group and there are not many characters aged over eighty in films or TV dramas. It seems to me that these days people over sixty are divided between those who try to pretend they are still young and can't face up to advancing age, and those of us who accept it, however reluctantly, and keep the core of their personality little changed. That's how I see it; I always refer to myself as a pensioner since that is what I am; nor am I one who is 'young at heart'. But I am not an old fogey, either. However, I do think that because the way young people look at the world today is often fundamentally different from the perspective of their grandparents, they are not likely to represent us with much insight, nor we them. [...]

I suppose government policy by its very nature is bound to be pretty inflexible and is never going to be able to cover needs within needs in any age group, especially in the near future. It is through 'whistle blowers', concerned members of the public and representations from charities that injustices may be exposed and, hopefully, alleviated. At present, the quality of government ministers does not inspire much confidence in the delivery of thoughtful policies.

Summer 2010, aged 83: Looking back over more than eighty years, I think the story of my life is that I always (starting as an only child) longed to belong. But I have rarely managed to fit in wherever I happened to be in company; now, at the end of my life, I have given up and go out of my way to avoid bonding. In the past I have been unhappy about feelings of isolation, but now I no longer mind.

When I moved to my present house in a typical inner London suburban Edwardian street, I thought perhaps at last I would get to know the residents and mix well with them, and so come to feel I belonged among them. But fifteen years later there has been no such happy outcome and I know almost no one in my street.

In old age I have become clumsy in my contacts with new people and have been less able than many of my contemporaries to absorb life style changes, in particular the present passion for shopping and spending. In other words, I don't fit well into the twenty-first century world. In this regard, the biggest gap in terms of belonging seems to me to be between the computer literate, with all the ramifications stemming from basic mastery, such as Apples, Blackberries, iPods – and the illiterate, or barely literate (me). I missed the start of the computer age and have never been able to catch up, and that shuts me out uncomfortable from all sorts of ways to communicate.

It has been an interesting life, but it ends with the biggest regret that of being an 'outsider'. One is the victim of one's personality!

Summer 2011, aged 84: I write this from the perspective of an eighty-four-year-old woman, watching herself gradually slipping into dependency which comes with extreme old age, but determined to resist it for as long as possible. And so far, I do manage to live with very little help and indeed to continue working on three half days each week, and to garden. I am comforted by the thought that when I can't do things for myself my family will look after me, for I live in the same house as my daughter and (at present) two grand-daughters in their twenties. However, my daughter will be sixty next year and the two girls are desperate for flats of their own. I live in a well-run borough and within fifteen minutes of our house are an excellent state-run nursing home and a terminal care home (hospice), one or other of which might be my destiny.

Now, thanks to the NHS offshoots of care homes; medicines seemingly offered to old people by the dosette boxful; ameliorative treatments for everything from hip and knee replacements to eye operations offered routinely; cancer and prostate cures; magazines such as *Saga* which cater for people of fifty upwards and are full of useful advice – everyone is, or can be, aware of old age and its problems in a manner that did not exist for my grandparents and much less than now even for my parents.

One old friend of mine has taken her life because she could see no point in continuing to endure constant pain and dependence on her husband and son to look after her. The one that I described above alternates [between] wanting her independence back with wanting to die, and I truly believe the kind of life she leads is completely pointless.

I have read that older people are often treated negligently in hospital, and when visiting I have sometimes seen meals placed where the patient can't easily reach them. The more feeble the patient, the less attention he/she seems likely to receive; whereas it should be the other way round. A few weeks ago I spent a night in the same hospital for hear[ing] tests, and even at eighty-four was treated as an intelligent person.

I am completely opposed to even a hint of privatization creeping into the NHS. The idea of hospitals being run for companies' profits is repugnant; the service should continue to be 'free at the point of supply' for anyone who needs it. I do think there is a lot wrong with the NHS in terms of the ratio of managers to professional doctors and nurses and I seriously think the return of matrons would do wonders to improve efficiency on the wards; I just don't understand the purpose of managers except for the procurement of supplies and services such as transport.

The current climate of severe budgetary cuts, coupled with the idea that old people want to remain in their own homes for as long as possible is beginning to make life very hard for many of them. They do of course receive visits, two or more a day in some cases, but that means many, many hours of lonely isolation for those who don't have children or grandchildren close at hand. This is the reverse of what one would hope to see in the future and makes a mock of 'care in the community'. To make things worse: the government's new policy of self-determination and grants in the form of 'personal budgets'.

Access and transport to day centres providing meals and stimulating activities for elderly men and women (pool and draughts for men, exercises and health talks for both sexes) make all the difference. I was involved in setting up such a centre thirty years ago, a registered charity which is now withering away because the economic climate is driving up prices to a level pensioners can't afford. So I see the immediate future as going backwards not forwards. Of course, if we spent less on armaments and wars (let alone the possible renewal of Trident) there would be more to spend on hospitals and services for the elderly.

What would be 'a good death'? A pain-free one, at home or in a hospice, with my daughter to hold my hand and myself in a frame of mind that acknowledges my life must end, however reluctantly, as one disengages from the future and leaves beloved people and places. Still in reasonably [good] health, for most of the time I find it hard to remember that my life's ending can't be far off; but then suddenly it hits me hard.

4

'Mine Has Been a Privileged Generation'

Dick Turpin

Dick Turpin *was born in London in 1930 and grew up in a working-class family in Tottenham. He is married with three children – including a late son – and lives in Sompting, West Sussex, where he raised his family. During the Second World War, Dick was evacuated from London and sent to live with his paternal grandparents in Stockport, Cheshire. In the late 1940s, he joined the army as a Royal Mechanical and Electrical Engineer. He took up six different postings over five years, including two-and-a-half years with the Rhine Army in Germany. He left when he felt a strong urge to settle down, 'find myself a wife and become a boring civilian'. Dick spent most of his working life in the motor trade and later worked as a local government transport officer. He also spent twelve years as a community Scout leader. Dick's younger brother committed suicide, and one of his sons was killed in a motorcycle accident at the age of twenty. He reflects on the devastating emotional impact of his son's death, and the grief that he and his wife continue to suffer. He believes the incident defined the rest of his life and connects it to supernatural experiences – such as finding his late son's cigarette butts in odd places.*

Dick describes himself as an 'old reactionary' with 'unfashionable' opinions: 'I am the kind of person that finds it difficult to hide my feelings. I am not inclined to take lectures from people about animal rights when they have a fag stuck between their fingers.' He disapproves of same-sex relationships, cohabitation before marriage, abortion and 'easy' divorce. Both his sons' marriages ended due to their wives' infidelities, and he is worried about how divorce will affect his grandchildren. Dick is cynical about the goals and achievements of the women's liberation movement and is bitterly opposed to the values of the younger generation – especially the 'modern mother'. 'Feminism has a lot to answer for,' he declares. Dick also writes extensively on the changing work environment. He cannot understand how anyone could find retirement boring. His own retirement is hectic with hobbies, tasks and grandchildren, and he enjoys not having the pressure to compete in the workforce. Dick feels that ageing is kinder on men, as they tend to become more attractive with age. His wife struggles with a chronic debilitating illness, and one of his grandchildren is severely disabled.

Aside from the three main directives discussed in the introduction and appendix of this book, the material in this chapter is also taken from replies to the following MO directives: 1994 'Death and Bereavement', 1998 'Staying Well and Everyday Life' and 2000 'Gays and the Family'.

Winter 1992, aged 62: For me life has definitely slowed down, but that is because I am now retired. Fortunately my savings and local government pension mean that there are no economic pressures upon me. So for the first time in my adult life I can enjoy the luxury of doing things in my own time. My pace of life now is about right. I would say my wife's poor health has slowed it down quite a bit. Fortunately my wife and I have managed our affairs sensibly and we are now in the happy position of being comfortably well off.

There is no doubt that for most people in full time employment the pace of life is still increasing. Even some unemployed people and school children find this to be the case. There are many reasons for this but I think the main reason is that for the last thirty years, young people have been emerging from the classroom with a much higher expectation of life. By now of course, in 1992, some of them are not so young. The teaching profession must have a lot of responsibility for this in the way they have encouraged young people to make demands of the adult population. Having to spend more time on paid work has been a feature of all my working life. Perhaps my generation were better prepared and equipped to make the most of our time and our lives. The only way I was going to get anything was by working for it.

Responsibility for children and elderly parents was the natural order of things for me; I cannot recall it being a burden. Perhaps I have been fortunate, especially in these modern times that my wife and I have been in agreement over such things. She was satisfied with the standard of living that one income produced and I was happy to spend my spare time with her and the children. As our parents grew older both the wife and I knew the debt we owed to them for giving us a happy and secure childhood. Caring for them in their old age was not a burden. Again perhaps we were fortunate in having elderly parents who took an interest in our lives and that of our children. They were happy to share our successes and (even in old age) willing to share our problems.

Now that I have more time to spare I can, for the first time in my life, enjoy the luxury of self-indulgence. I do things simply because I feel like doing them. Mass Observation is an example of my interests. I enjoy putting my thoughts on paper. How much credibility researchers give them is another matter. Since I have retired I have become interested in family history, a much more absorbing interest than I thought it would be. Perhaps I am lucky having so many hobbies. I certainly have not encountered boredom since I have been retired.

Photography and tapestry are two more of my hobbies. These days I allot a period of time each day to a particular activity, that way I never get fed up with things.

Again I have been fortunate in coping with the emotions and health aspects of pressure. I have a volatile personality and I am inclined to erupt in an outburst of anger when things upset me too much. Fortunately my wife is a very understanding person. Her usual reaction after an explosion is 'Do you feel better now?' Usually I do. It also seems to work wonders for my blood pressure and heart. Medical checks always record a rock steady heart beat and a very normal blood pressure. Perhaps there is a message there; I am certainly not the type to let things build up forever.

I remember a few years ago asking a service engineer who was looking at a pressure washer I had bought for the council from a German manufacturer. 'How do you like working for a German company?' I asked. 'Smashing', he replied, 'for the first time in my life I am somebody'. That conversation says it all. If I had my time over again I would be a politician or a criminal. Sarcastic? Well my wife and I come from a large circle of family relatives representing something like thirty family groups. The only family group that does not seem to be bothered by redundancy or the threat of unemployment or repossession includes a nephew whose profession is house breaker! That unfortunately says more about the state of Britain in the spring of 1992 than any amount of words.

I frequently read of people in my own age group being described as elderly. It irritates me immensely. I just do not think of myself in such a fashion, getting on a bit maybe, elderly, never! The word suggests one is past it, over the hill just waiting to kick the bucket. There is still plenty of life left in me. Old?! Well I suppose there does come a time, if we are lucky, when we have to admit that we are over the hill. Perhaps we all know when that time has come; perhaps I might be able to accept it gracefully.

A lot of young people are beginning to learn the lessons of life when they're aged thirty-plus, many of them the hard way. By the time they are forty they have become categorized: those who have learned the lessons of life, and those who probably never will. I think most of them become politicians, the dimmest of them cabinet ministers. My fifties were the best years of my life. The mortgage was paid off, the children were grown up. My career had been reasonably successful, my wife was earning an income and we were able to enjoy ourselves and all the good things that had been beyond us when we were raising a family. Now that I am in my sixties I have had to cope with an enforced early retirement (which I bitterly resented) and unfortunately my wife's poor health.

I have thought for many years that older people are too demanding and selfish these days. Now that I am retired myself I can put such thoughts on paper. In many ways mine has been a privileged generation. We enjoyed the benefit of thirty years of full employment after the Second World War. I was not only able to choose which trade I was apprenticed to, but which company's apprenticeship offer I would accept.

In my view most people retiring now have had ample opportunity to provide for their old age. That is those who did not make too many demands on life. People today do not believe me when I tell them it took me almost ten years to earn my first thousand pounds. For something like 95% of my working life I earned substantially less than the much vaunted 'average wage'. Even when I retired in 1990 as a senior officer in local government my salary was less than £15,000 a year. Yet I have no mortgage and no debts. My wife and I do not live like lords, but we are comfortable. To demand more would be to add to the burden of taxation for those who can least afford it.

In my life time the greatest burden of financial deprivation was when my wife and I were supporting a family of three young sons. Our income per head of family was always well below the basic old age pension. I think that situation is just as true today, and I am sure that young people in that situation have no more sympathy for grasping old fogeys than I had. Perhaps my generation was better equipped to handle that stage in life. We had not been brainwashed in the classroom to think the world owed us a living. In fact the opposite was the case. We did not think expensive cars, exotic holidays etc. were life's essentials.

For me there have been considerable gains in getting older. I suppose throughout history young men have felt the need to compete with their contemporaries to establish their niche in society. We all want the promotions to better paid jobs, we all want to survive when redundancy threatens, we all want the trimmings of success. In the army, who would be the first young soldier to win a stripe? As I got older I was happy to find that I did not need to be so subservient to those who had power over me. I'm happy to be free of the need to compete without, so far, having to pay much of a price. My age is not a burden to me yet.

I did resent it when the Council made me redundant. Especially when I knew it was a contrived redundancy, as I had embarrassed the politicians. I resented the suggestion that my working life was over. In fact I resented it so much I went out and took the first job that was offered to me, even though it was working for peanuts, just to prove I could get a job and hold it down. I did not mind so much when that job folded up twelve months later. Recently I have been recruited as a part-time member of the sales team of an importer of municipal machinery. He thinks my local government experience has a value. That means something to me.

1994, aged 64: Born just eighteen years after the Great War, evidence of its effect upon people was all around me. The disabled and mutilated survivors of that conflict were part of my childhood. As soon as I was able to remember I shared the two minutes silence on Armistice Day to remember the dead, and two minutes is a very long time for a small and active boy. The thought of dying itself does not bother me much. I presume that is something to do with my age. Now aged sixty-three, I know I cannot look beyond the next two decades and I am not sure that I want to.

My father – aged eighty-two when he died – had decided he did not want to live any longer. Senility was setting in and he did not want to go on. He willed himself to die. The wife and I have made no special arrangements for our demise. I think it is a rather morbid thought. When our son was killed on his motor bike we paid for a grave that would accommodate us two when we died. So long as there is enough money in our estate to do that we are not bothered.

I have had some unusual experiences at times when tragic deaths have occurred in my family. My brother's suicide at the age of twenty was a traumatic time for all the family. I had a girlfriend of sorts at the time and she dropped me soon afterwards, which did not help. My mother nearly went out of her mind and never fully recovered. She had to be heavily sedated, especially at night. One night, heavily drugged, she began to sing to my brother with the voice of a young woman just as she had done when he was a baby. I went upstairs to her room, took her hand in mine and prayed. She settled down to a peaceful night's sleep.

My son was killed in a traffic accident in France. In response to a phone call from the French police my wife and I, with the parents of his companion, caught the overnight ferry from Newhaven to Dieppe. We travelled there to the village where the accident happened by taxi and in the early hours of the morning were brutally told, outside a locked up police station, that our son was dead. It was like a physical blow of such ferocity that all self-control was lost. I cried like a child. Eventually we arrived at a hotel and a doctor gave me an injection. I woke up at daylight to a beautiful late September sunny morning. Heavy droplets of dew on the grass reflected the rays of the morning sun. My son was a lover of nature and would have been delighted with such a morning.

'The first day of Thomas's holiday', I thought, 'and he is dead, finished'. Yet even as I harboured the thought rejection of it came upon me. 'Thomas is not finished, he goes on'.

Psychiatrists might say that the thought of my son, who I dearly loved, being finished was just too awful for my subconscious mind to accept. All I can say is that I was thinking one thing when the conviction that the complete opposite was the case came upon me, and I believe that conviction came from an external source. I have never doubted that conviction since.

It was a disappointment to us when Thomas took up smoking, but being a thoughtful lad he never smoked indoors knowing how it upset his mother's asthma. To keep the cost of his smoking down he rolled his own cigarettes, being frugal with the tobacco he put in them. At the bottom of the garden outside the greenhouse we had bought for him as a boy was an accumulation of Thomas's weeds. A painful reminder of the considerate son we had lost.

I had to clear them up and swept the paths round the area, yet every time I went down the garden I found the remains of at least one of Thomas's weeds. I cleared the area more thoroughly, even searching adjacent plant and flower beds to make sure I had not missed any, but I still kept finding them. We all found it difficult to accept any supernatural explanation for the events. Then the day came and I went down to the garden to water the greenhouse and there floating on top of the water butt was one of Thomas's weeds. The next day I found the last one on the staging in his greenhouse. I can offer no explanation for these events – only that I had never found any of Thomas's weeds in the water butt or the greenhouse before, or since!

Christmas that year was just three months after the death of my son and neither my wife nor myself felt like celebrating. But we had two other sons and felt we ought to make the effort for them. We did not put up any decorations but bought a small potted Christmas tree. Thomas had always been a lover of nature and hated anything artificial. If we had a tree it had to be a real one. We have never dared to put artificial flowers on his grave. The tree was duly decorated and placed in the lounge where the tree had always been at Christmas. Christmas morning I got up and went into the lounge. The room immediately struck me as being filled with the presence of Thomas. 'He has been to see his tree', I said to my wife.

'I know', she replied.

There is of course nothing tangible in all these events. They could be easily explained as the imaginings of a sad old man unable to accept the finality of his son's death. There would be no point trying to persuade me that was the case.

1998, aged 68: Everyone tells me I am remarkably fit and active for my age and indeed I do seem to be just as energetic as men twenty years younger than myself. I can keep up with younger men when doing D.I.Y. jobs but I do have a few aches and pains when I finish. Knowing when to stop and rest is a matter of judgement. It usually comes with age and experience and if you don't know when by the time you're my age you never will. Yes wear and tear is a natural part of getting older but it need not unduly influence the way we live. One has to accept that limbs do stiffen up after a while and that playing with the grandchildren has its price. Again it comes back to one's attitude and response to these conditions. A positive response is always a great help and certainly helps to come to terms with one's difficulties.

I find that those who do not readily give in to aches and pains cope with them best. My wife's illness can at times cause her a great deal of distress, yet she does not complain. It is only by observing her movements and her drawn features that I know her condition is more painful than usual.

Chronic illness is the most difficult to come to terms with. My wife has *spondalitis*, a fusing of the bones in the spine and rib cage, and *polymiliga rhumatica*, an arthritic condition of the bloodstream. Both conditions cannot be cured only hopefully contained. They can be extremely painful and disabling and fluctuate from being uncomfortable to intensely painful. It does amaze me sometimes how well my wife copes and is so cheerful most of the time ... something that constantly surprises those who are treating her. Sometimes she can be a bit weepy; especially when she thinks about how her illness has frustrated the plans we made for our retirement. But I would not change her. The love we share is the most precious thing of all. I am convinced her positive response not only helps her to cope but also helps her body resist the worst effects of her illness. A shining example to those who would let illness wear them down.

2000, aged 70: I feel feminism has a lot to answer for. The advocates seem to have little regard for the consequences of what they do. The young women my sons have partnered have had no qualms about ending a relationship or even a marriage so that they can embark on another affair. They have not cared who they hurt, even their own children. The partners they now live with tolerate their children because they must. They have no affection for them or interest in their welfare. There is no doubt that my grandchildren are unhappy growing up in such an environment and it upsets my wife greatly.

To my mind, women themselves will become the greatest victims of their 'liberation'. My wayward ex-daughter-in-laws are not happy women. They know what they have done, and one in particular is always seeking to justify what she has done. The men they have taken up with are nothing like as considerate or gentle as my sons were. In fact I think they are both being used. They seem to be stuck in a situation they cannot get out of. And as far as I am concerned it serves them right. Thirty years from now there are going to be a lot of poor and lonely old women around. I cannot see how it can be otherwise. Children grow up, I know. Then their mothers will have no more claim on the pockets of my sons, or the taxpayer. Another thing we can be certain of, when the time comes, the advocates of feminism, like all pressure group activists, will not want to know about picking up the bill.

There is no doubt that my sons were very much in need of parental support when their marriages broke up. It is for so many young men a frustrating and depressing experience. They were brought up to believe a marriage was for life. They had not wanted extra-marital affairs and had not sort to evade their obligations as husbands and fathers. But in this day and age, when things go wrong it is the husband who loses everything and has to start again. Especially when there are children involved. My oldest son in particular lost everything he had worked for fifteen years. Just so that his wife could have an affair. That was late twentieth-century justice. It makes me angry when I hear of people talk about no fault divorce.

Autumn 2006, aged 76: These days middle age seems to last to the verge of retirement. Then one becomes getting on a bit. Old age is not really due to start these days until one is on the wrong side of eighty. Though in my experience there are plenty who are seventy plus who would disagree with that. Where do I position myself? At seventy-six coming up seventy-seven: old.

In my experience we cannot deny the passing of the years. No matter how hard we try. I had a mother who tried very hard. To me, especially in my youth, she was an embarrassment. It does seem to me that in this modern age people seem reluctant to leave the frivolities of youth behind them as the years progress. There is a marked reluctance to grow up. Our present Prime Minister [Tony Blair], with his juvenile attraction to pop artists and the world of entertainment, exemplifies this trend for me. Which is why he is such a disaster.

As a young man I assumed that by the time I was fifty the best part of my life would be behind me and that I would have no interest in things like sex. I should have known better. My parents had enjoyed good holidays and an active social life at that age. My father worked away from home a lot and I fancy more than one landlady took a shine to him. I suspect it was a thought that bothered mother too.

In some respects our fifties were a golden age for my wife and myself. Our sons were finished with university and college. The mortgage was paid off and for the first time in twenty-five years we had money to spare. Holidays abroad, two holidays a year even, we even splashed out on a new car. Several new cars in fact. Our golden decade did not last long into my sixties. As a service manager in local government it was inevitable that I would become a victim of Thatcherism. I did when I was sixty, and we lost two thirds of our income. Our son's matrimonial problems were very expensive. Divorce court judges have no qualms about giving away the end product of a man's life time of work to a wayward wife. For my wife and myself the sixties became a very stressful and expensive decade. A contrived redundancy, stressful divorces, distressed grandchildren, and a catalogue of health problems. My wife having to have a hysterectomy, followed by a deep vein thrombosis, and then four heart attacks ending with open heart by-pass surgery. She was too obstinate to die.

As a young man I did not think much about being beyond the age of seventy, though three of my four grandparents had lived well beyond that age. If I did have any assumptions it would have been about pottering in the garden, eking out a pension and not enjoying any great prosperity. My seventies were very much a continuation of my sixties, though one begins to become aware that the time clock is ticking away. I am the sole survivor of the family I grew up in. Many of my relations and neighbours do not seem to be coping well with the problems of old age. I sometimes wonder if all our trials and tribulations have done us a favour. Both my wife and myself are still very active and happily self-reliant. Which, believe me, when I observe the plight of my less fortunate contemporaries is a great blessing.

Everyone today seems to have greater expectations for their retirement. I think politicians in the past have been dishonest in encouraging such expectations. In the first instance the state pension was designed to keep people out of the workhouse. That is, put a roof over their head, a meal on the table, and a shirt on their back. Nothing more. People today expect a lot more than that and with people living so much longer they are costly and quite unattainable expectations. Especially when we consider what demands other groups make of the economy.

I have never given much thought to life beyond the age of eighty. There is a common misconception that life can still be a ball beyond that age. Only for the very fortunate few. In fact it is a time when all kinds of infirmity begin to become a burden and people's minds begin to fade. I am convinced my father willed himself to die at the age of eighty-one. He had become very infirm and began to hallucinate. Always an intelligent and capable man he decided it was time to go.

Not having to get up for work in the morning is the big gain, though even that can take some getting used to. Some find it difficult to accept becoming yesterday's man. I did, though it was the circumstances of my becoming such that made it difficult for me to accept. My career in local government blossomed late in life and I was not ready to be put out to grass at the tender age of sixty. On the other hand, provided one can live comfortably on a pension, it can be a relief to be out of the rat race. No longer having to guard your back against those who would harm you in order to prosper their own ambitions ... as I eventually concluded.

Winter 2009, aged 79: I do not read many books that are set in the present day. I sometimes start to read a modern story serialized in my newspaper. I usually get fed up with it long before the end, especially if it is what is called a misery memoir. Everyone seems to have been sexually abused in childhood these days. I do not sympathize with what I see as petty concerns of this modern age. As a child of the thirties my ideas of poverty and misery are a great deal different. I come from a large nuclear family. My father was an engineering craftsman, as his father was before him. My uncles were mechanics, factory hands, painters, bus conductors, barbers, cobblers. The ideas and values I acquired in such a family environment have no place in twenty-first century society ...

It seems to me the thoughts and feelings of my age group become ever less important. Inevitable I suppose. Is this the case with other age groups too? Difficult for me to say. I'm afraid I see younger people as the 'me' or 'I want' generations ... It is the way they have been educated. There is a distinct difference in the ideas of my age group and those who have grown up since the end of the Second World War. The Welfare State has influenced ideas and values more than is generally thought.

Writers and politicians seek brownie points in addressing the problems of the old – though they all balk at the expenses of addressing such issues. The truth is: today's pensioners are the most pampered ever. Most of us spent almost all our working lives in the post-war era of full employment. I may not have lived off the fat of the land, but I have never known what it is to be unemployed. Sadly my oldest grandchildren, barely out of their teens know more about it than I do.

Can I think of any representations of my age group in the media or government policy that seems to show stereotypes? The word pensioner seems to suggest to people fragile and confused old people unable to cope any more. Yet most of my contemporaries are still sharp as a button. I suspect it might surprise researchers to discover how many of us have at some time had to come to the aid of adult offspring who have got themselves into a mess. Sometimes even adult grandchildren.

I sometimes think Bruce Forsyth has a bit of an edge when he, in jest of course, keeps asserting he is not doddery. Doddery he is not! Ageism is another word that comes to mind. Especially when campaigners keep on about older drivers. Yet every year when my car insurance is due I am inundated with mail shots from insurance companies wanting my business. So I must be doing something right. I am sure I was a victim of ageism and target chasing policeman when they decided to prosecute me over an incident involving me and a sports car driver on a roundabout in Worthing (despite the claims of the other driver not standing up to examination, and the statement of his own witness contradicting his own statement to the police). Even my solicitor did not think I stood a chance. My acquittal of all charges and the award of full costs against the CPS says it all.

It also irritates me intensely when government spokesmen whinge about the cost of pensions, which most of my generation worked and paid for, for fifty years, and which in my case is taxed, and the demands we make of the NHS. Weekend binge drinkers make infinitely more demands than I do, and as far as I can see most of them are unemployed. Probably unemployable!

I do not think governments are all that interested in stereotypes or complex notions [of old age]. Only those most likely to favour their party. Having worked in local government for twenty-seven years, a working environment very much subject to the whims of politicians. I am convinced they are only interested in the party's and their own fortunes and their own particular brand of political dogma. Politics is a career and those who make it theirs are most interested in number one.

5

'Rushing About'

Beryl Saunders

Beryl Saunders *was born in 1931. She is now registered blind. Her former jobs include full-time social work for an adoption agency and part-time counselling (post-adoption and egg donation). She has also worked as a landlady for a B&B. Her marriage to an accountant ended after eighteen years due to infidelity, and she was single for a further eighteen years before living with her present lover. She struggles to find age-appropriate vocabulary to describe her romantic partner ('lover', 'partner' and 'boyfriend' don't seem suitable). She has a colourful romantic history and writes extensively on marriage, sex, contraception and intimate family relationships. She feels that the stereotype of older people not enjoying love and sex is 'an arrogant and ignorant assumption'. Beryl writes frankly about menopause and midlife 'changeability'.*

While she is open to using the internet, she finds printed and digital media difficult due to her poor eyesight and prefers to receive news and information verbally. While she was once an avid reader, she is now restricted to audio books. 'I didn't feel old until I began to lose my sight', she writes. 'Slowly I'm more dependent on my partner, who, like many men, becomes sillier and less responsible with ageing. I must bite back my annoyance, knowing I need to ask him to read even the instructions on a tin!' She describes the 'dreaded Elderly Manner' in detail and reflects intelligently on representations of older people in the media.

Aside from the three main directives discussed in the introduction and appendix of this book, the material in this chapter is also taken from replies to the following MO directive: 2009 'Mid-life Transitions'.

Winter 1992, aged 62: I have just retired this week from a very busy schedule as social worker in the adoption and fostering section of an inner city area. It was a demanding job with a lot of evening and weekend work, much mileage covered in the car going about visiting families. My partner Tom has been retired for two years, so he has to get used to having me at home all day.

As we don't have clear ideas about the purpose of life it is hard to know whether we lose out by rushing about, or by sagging about. I have a friend, Mabel, a retired psychologist aged 65, who is never happy unless her diary is crammed tight with appointments – often involving several drives a week from London to Devon and back. When Mabel retired she was so afraid she would feel empty that she booked for eight evening classes a week by mistake. She never has time to clean her house, which is choc-a-bloc with carrier bags filled with newspaper cuttings. She spends a fortune on therapy: aroma therapy, massage, group therapy – in an effort to counteract stress. Because she is so overloaded she is very forgetful, and has to write herself lots of notes and reminders which she then loses. She spends hours hunting for them among the plastic carrier bags.

I love Mabel, but find her frustrating in some ways. She causes me to observe that not only may I feel dissatisfied with the pace of my OWN life, but I am critical of the pace at which others live as well! I am quite cautious, and quite anxious, not to 'do a Mabel' or 'do a Phil' in this time of retirement. It seems like a 'last chance' to get things right in terms of life satisfaction. When I'm dying I want to be able to look back over, say, 20 years of my retirement and feel fulfilled – but what does this mean? How much structure is needed to enable me to fulfil my wishes, how much structure should I be prepared to dismantle if it is all getting too rigid? So far I have had some days when I have drifted from job to job like a little breeze flapping here and there, and at the end of the day I've thought, 'My God, what have I achieved today'? Other days I've got up, programmed: 'today I'll do this in the morning, this in the afternoon, this in the evening'. What I find is that it doesn't matter which kind of day I've accomplished – it is how I feel that matters.

I suddenly have all day to do jobs I used to cram into a Saturday or Sunday. Hundreds of times I've thought 'once I retire I'll … clean out that cupboard, read that book, use that modelling clay, take that study course, keep the car clean, write to those old friends, rearrange that bedroom, reorganise my filing system, go to that theatre/cinema/art gallery/stately home/bargain basement'. Idiotically, in the first short days of retirement I've spent some time rushing from one of these activities to another, saying 'Now you KNOW you said you'd do it when you retired, so get on and DO IT' (as though there was a recording angel sitting somewhere with a well-worn notebook jotting down 'she STILL hasn't done that'). Other days I've done just one small thing and taken my time over it and really enjoyed it, but who knows which is right.

So at this very moment my life is a series of false starts and false stops while I feel my way and try to learn new ideas about pace.

I didn't mention that besides being a social worker I have done bed and breakfast for 8 years. Up till now this has been mostly at the weekends. Being a bed and breakfast landlady often implies spending frilly little bits of time tuning in to the needs and wishes of the guest of the moment – listening with the inner eye just to get a sense of how to deal with them. This is always fun and always worthwhile, however varied the guests and however peculiar.

Another thing I never see as a waste of time, whatever the punishing schedule, is to stop and make love. My partner and I are very keen on sex. The fact that time becomes timeless during lovemaking, during periods of horror or great happiness, contradicts everything said so far about the pace of life, because again, somehow, it comes back to a perceived pace rather than something actual.

The mind-wandering I used to do when driving has now largely been replaced by mind-wandering while cleaning and bed-making. Though now and again, since retirement, I have noticed some sort of 'car-deprivation' coming on. I can usually organize a shopping trip to another town or a visit to a not too near Garden Centre to get in the necessary day-dreaming.

Given my age and my new found freedom I should say at this very moment the pace of my life is too slow and there are copious plans for absorbing time and energy. I am in the process of setting up as an independent infertility counsellor. It is quite hard pushing against the inertia of having yet another easy day to get on with preparing leaflets, sorting out a mailing list and beginning to advertise. My goal is the Autumn – by then I hope to be engaged in seeing clients, say, three days a week. That still gives me four days for the bed and breakfast, leisure and further study.

I've spent most of the last 20 years working. Social work isn't something that ends at 5 p.m. Even once I got home there were sometimes phone calls from foster or adoptive parents in the evenings – once or twice in the middle of the night ... Well, now I'm in the position of being able to choose my timetable. I intend to see clients in my home, probably 3 days a week maximum ... I have the last word about taking bed and breakfast guests.

Since I retired I have time to do things in the garden which I left entirely to my partner before. I'm not sure how he feels about my being out there pottering about, it could be rather irritating for him.

I'm 61 and I can't really believe it – I still 'feel the same inside' as I did when I was 20 ... Reluctantly I have to place myself amongst the elderly: I have my bus pass (and jolly useful it is too). One watershed is the greying of the hair, and/or balding. If I go into a room and all I see around me are grey heads, I tend to assume I'm in a gathering of the elderly. For one awful moment I stereotype the lot, forgetting, honestly, that I am among their number. If I'm driving behind somebody who doesn't know our moorland roads and they're dithering along, I see a grey head, and think 'Aha, a wrinkly Sunday driver' – extremely unjust.

It's been lucky for me that I still have not one grey hair. I think that it is helpful for me in 'going independent' rather than being 'retired'. I am setting up 2 businesses since I finished full-time work.

There are some quite fatal ingredients of the 'elderly' manner which I have watched and noted carefully since I joined that group myself (determining of course to avoid the obvious pitfalls) ... Some of the ingredients of this dreaded Elderly Manner are: fussiness and agitation (both physical and mental), constantly digging into a handbag, losing purse and change, losing your ticket, hankie etc., losing your specs and car keys eight or nine times a day, and getting fussed about it ... All the physical fidgeting that goes with this. Minding too much about temporary comfort and discomfort (draughts etc.) and making a song and dance about it. Worrying about bus times, train times, whether the waitress has noticed you etc.

A lot of the tendencies listed above are habits which can be guarded against (with a bit of self-awareness and some self-control). I can feel myself beginning to do them and I can also stop it. Another aspect of this way of behaving is deliberately getting out of date: saying 'I can't manage these new-fangled videos, coffee-machines, word-processors, faxes, cheque cards, electric kettles' ... you name it. Unless somebody's intelligence or manual ability has severely deteriorated through ill-health, they can actually manage all these things, and others if they want to.

Perhaps the most aging factor of all is the steady, quiet, unaware curtailing of interest, and interests, until some old people seem literally boxed in, mentally. I am not talking about the effects of ill-health, which people can't help, but the steady eroding of interest in anything outside one's own little 'patch' – geographical and mental. Again, as with the physical fidgetiness and anxiety, a lot of it is habit. It is important for older people to keep up to date by mixing with every age group, by reading, noticing what goes on TV and radio, but above all by listening to other people and exchanging ideas, rather than just information.

The 60s should be a time of release from old patterns, and an opportunity to look at how you want to be as a person in the last 20 years of your life. For many people, freedom from the grindstone is an enhancing experience, but there are plenty of people who just don't know what to do with themselves. When they've polished their house to the nth degree and tidied their garden, they can only think of a visit to the shops or bingo, or another session in front of the TV to fill their time.

There needs to be a level of acceptance that there will be things that will never now be achieved, but there can also be the challenge of taking up something entirely new and learning and developing. There is still time for another burst of education or learning a new skill. For a lot of people this is a time when they undertake or extend a range of voluntary work.

For some people the 60s shows the first signs of ill-health or disability that is going to be a major affliction as the years go by. How they respond to it now may affect their future.

70s – by this age some individuals are 'really old', crawling along, bent double, sick, lonely, possibly bereaved of a loved partner, running on little tramlines or habit and routine. Others are enjoying the rich rewards and fruits of life: 'Honour, love, obedience, troops of friends', and have the joy of being turned to by friends and family for their wisdom, compassion and experience. Sadly, most people in their 70s are not like this; too many have shrunk, physically, mentally and emotionally, but some are. What a joy it is to encounter such people. Of course I imagine I shall be like this myself, but who knows. My father was, until 5 days before his death at 79.

So, people in their 70s should be actively preparing for death. There is 'unfinished business' in most people's lives; now is the time to face it squarely, and sort it out where possible. There must be regrets over mistakes, failures, disappointments and injustices. They need an honourable acknowledgement within. Some goodbyes need saying. By the time a person is 70 some contemporaries will already be gone. There is a certain smugness about not having died, but there is also the gap left by old friends, some of whom have been friends from childhood.

Autumn 2006, aged 75: I regard myself as old …

With luck, following retirement there's a good period of freedom, busyness, activity before one really begins to feel old. As they say *60 is the new 40*. People of 60 still have the world at their feet so long as they enjoy good health.

I loved the first ten years after retiring from social work because constant evening work, so much immersion in other people's lives had left me too weary to participate in local activities, spend time with friends.

Suddenly at 62 I had time to enjoy brief sessional work carried out on *my* terms, to attend classes, take extra bed and breakfast guests, again at *my* pace, spend time with my partner with days out. Most importantly to undertake voluntary counselling with a Post-Adoption agency that built on my previous expertise, but where I had the *luxury* of giving adequate time to each client.

I did not feel old, made more friends in the immediate vicinity than I would have thought possible, joined a choir and started on some medium term, paid, writing projects.

It is health that matters; I didn't feel old until I began to lose my sight. Other respondents will certainly cite equally disabling health problems. Suddenly the voluntary job to which I'd given so much was no longer possible – for it depended heavily on accessing and interpreting old adoption records. Book reviews, another mainstay, could no longer be undertaken.

Men and women: It's a generalization that the friendship patterns of men differ from those of women – they are more dependent on casual groups:

work colleagues, sport/interest. Close one to one friendships are not so common. Therefore retirement particularly, and old age generally, leave them more stranded. Less accustomed to multi-tasking without a strong hobby a man has less structure to his time. He's lucky if he does possess a dominant interest. He may be brilliant in one or two areas, but incapable of taking an overall view.

My partner is (and coincidentally my father was) an absolute marvellous gardener, can produce beauty and effect, and persevere till things are done. But this comes at a price – he is completely unaware what goes on in the rest of our household; is genuinely amazed if I say *the bin men come today, better get the rubbish out*. Domestically dyslexic, he just cannot envisage the sequence of events necessary for a job to be done, i.e. washing/drying/ironing/airing/putting away.

Gains and losses: Retirement has many, many advantages, but real old age has few. Old age is the price we pay for having made it this far. Briefly here are some disadvantages:-

The imminence of death …

The loss of loved ones …

Lack of energy …

Slowing down …

Shortage of money: Women in my generation qualified for small pensions only, having spent years at home with our children. After retirement when the time comes when a pension can no longer be supplemented by part-time earnings it withers away. I was shocked to learn that together my partner and myself are below the poverty line. Yet disability brings a mass of small extra expenses. There is of course financial or practical help for the elderly blind, though people imagine there is some sort of benefit.

Part of the anxiety simply caused by ageing is because one is more easily upset anyway – so the arrival of a bill or the appearance of the meter reader brings a sinking of the heart.

Because we have a quaint and interesting house we may look comfortable because we have savings we dip into them to meet daily expenses. One day they will be gone. We gather from this week's news that if we ever need care we must pay – do we sell the house to meet care costs for me, or for him – is one partner to be left without a home?

No car: many older people are forced to stop driving for practical, health or because of financial considerations. Then life contracts violently for services, amenities, entertainments, shops are all geared towards the car user. Public transport may get us from A to B but takes 3 times as long, is unreliable, and rarely goes where we want. For instance few of my friends live alongside a bus stop or train station. We've lost all those happy days visiting gardens and places of interest.

Nowadays, shopping must be carried home, the Big Shop a thing of the past ...

Yes, car loss is the most serious disadvantage of ageing.

A small problem of age-related disability is the near-impossibility of getting the right help. It is cumbersome to explain one's exact needs. For instance, I still have peripheral vision, so can get about but I do better if I walk behind another. Yet people insist on ushering me through every doorway first. Because they see me getting about it never occurs to them that when we get to the pub I can't read the menu, find the loo.

Advantages?

Friendships ...

Grandchildren are a joy for some, not for me, since I have none. I observe friends, deeply involved, loving it, others overwhelmed by the amount of support they need to provide, perhaps to single parents.

Memories ...

Radio and audio books ...

'When I am old I shall wear purple'– as Jenny Joseph famously enunciated – I no longer care what people think of my appearance, actions, what I say. I'm no longer afraid to address a meeting, sing a solo, recite, crack a joke in a dismal silence – my privilege.

An extension of the above = freedom of thought, absence of shame. If I want to gaze yearningly at a gorgeous young man, relish lustful fantasies, I may in the privacy of my head. Once I feared thoughts showed in my face. Now, who cares! I'm invisible anyway. People assume the elderly aren't interested in sex – far from the truth, which my partner would joyfully endorse.

Mustn't forget the free bus pass – local only and the free TV license, half price at the cinema and concessions at adult classes. It's not all bad.

Winter 2009, aged 78: For many women of my mother's generation the menopause must have represented a mighty relief from anxiety about further pregnancies and not signalled the end of sexual activity. Certainly among current friends plenty continue to enjoy sexual activity well into their 70s. Others very clearly do not – separate bedrooms are explained away by insomnia or snoring, wind even.

My experience ... At the age of 46 I had been divorced six years and was enjoying my independence – own flat, no longer humbly occupying the erstwhile matrimonial home, both children at college – employed as a social worker in Surrey, plenty of friends, leisure activities, one or two light-hearted affairs, I didn't envisage big changes.

Suddenly, out of the blue I fell violently in love with a married man from Yorkshire who pursued me intensely after we met at a sexuality workshop – part of the Encounter movement fashionable at the time. He pursued me energetically by phone and during business trips to Surrey.

We began an intense affair. Initially I regarded it as similar to my previous entanglements. After all I was happy with my current lifestyle and friendships [...]

To cut a long story short I lost all caution, sold everything and obtained a high status social work post in Yorkshire ... within months. Some friends said I was mad, other applauded my taking a chance on love. When I arrived in Yorkshire, the ghastly winter or 1979 came upon us, snow for months – no phone, inessential car journeys a no-no. I didn't see, scarcely heard from my lover for months. When I did it transpired that he was unnerved by my appearance, seeing me as a threat to his marriage. Our relationship tailed off over the next twelve months. Was this his mid life crisis, or mine? I had apparently disrupted my children's lives and removed myself from close friendships in Guildford for no purpose. Mad.

But I did not regret this transition long term as I loved my new job and love Yorkshire.

Interesting, the physical manifestations didn't appear for two years, hence my inability to recognize the menopausal when it began. I suffered several years of violent, almost constant bleeding which proved exhausting and embarrassing [...]

After the birth of two unplanned children in her forties, my mother rather pointedly directed my father to the spare bedroom, and he was not encouraged to return! Probably quite a common scenario for their generation – they would kiss goodnight at the bedroom door.

Prostrate malfunction is common among older men – is this linked with hormonal reduction? It's not for nothing that Viagra has enjoyed so much publicity. I had several affairs with men in their mid/late fifties who while basically loyal to their marriages appeared critical or nervous of their wives' dwindling sexual appetites.

There is a madness around which attempts to deny such natural, biological changes which have an evolutionary purpose. HRT, Viagra, IVF well past the natural limits, cosmetic surgery, serial partnerships, toy boys and dolly birds are some ingredients in this denial, inept on the whole.

Winter 2009, aged 78: My experience: I can no longer read more than a few words at a time – because I have lost my central vision, each word has to be located separately. Large print makes some slight difference with short texts like letters. I haven't managed any kind of book for some 7 years.

It's assumed all blind people use Braille, but I doubt that individuals who have lost their sight in old age feel like embarking on mastering a complex and exhausting technique. The main reason we need to read is to obtain information:- shopping, public transport, town centres, all kinds of instructions – none of these categories would be improved by knowing Braille. I'm fed up with being asked if I've learned Braille – struggling with the non-availability of quite ordinary information every single day.

Enquirers wrongly assume my greatest loss is not being able to sit down with the latest Booker Prize volume. Not so – it is the absence of information that inflames the visually impaired. As for fiction – it can be accessed in audio format, although only 4% of a published material is available thus …

So, my reading experience is limited to the four percent. I belong to *Calibre* a wonderful postal service for people unable to read …

Why must I explain again and again that I can't access the audio book section in the library, for instance – not set out to suit the visually impaired.

I've always loved reading – a book on the go since the age of 8. Rather frowned upon by my parents' generation … I still keep at least one audio book on the go today … I read novels, classics, including old favourites …

Whether books give a better account of characters and events than other media is an impossible question. The novelist's task differs from that of the reporter or the very ephemeral entertainment provided by TV. The novelist sets out to communicate the events and viewpoint of an individual, or group within an individual setting. It is therefore essential that the reader is persuaded to enter into their lives – that depends on the writer's skill and the reader's response to their specific style. We respond differently to different authors.

Talking about books: Here sight loss is a handicap as I'm unlikely to be reading anything friends are talking about – they'll all be on recent award winners and new publications. I used to discuss books all the time, less nowadays.

Most of my friends belong to different book groups, or attend literature classes. Book groups rarely select material available in audio, it'd be a one off if they did, and I wouldn't know about it …

But who can fail to enjoy a relaxed discussion among friends? I recently had *Small Island* by Andrea Levy on CD and was lucky enough to hear her interviewed on Woman's Hour, also share impressions with a couple of friends. Rare for me these days.

However, reverting to my sighted days, some 8 years ago I joined a book group at the local library, about 10 members. My memories may not be superbly accurate by now. Book choice was in the hands of the librarian and influenced by novels available in quantity. The group met monthly, frequent enough for me; I enjoyed tackling works I wouldn't normally have considered. However meetings were chaired, most ineptly by a very nice woman nobody liked to criticise; they were completely unstructured and quickly degenerated into a free for all. The librarian proved so eager to be democratic, that no opinion was challenged, nor was discussion focused under headings … It was at this level: *Did you like it? Yes/No. It was rubbish.* No reasons, no analysis, no reflection, a few loud mouths dominated, irritating. I stuck with it because it was local …

When I could see I attended more literary festivals than is now possible. I regularly drove to Ilkley – quite a prestigious festival, which provided a rich programme – events mostly organized in the evening however which involved a long late drive home – couldn't do it now …

My age group: I don't think one can compare treatment in fiction with media coverage or Government reports. The writers' aims are so different. As a pensioner I am certainly sick of the portrayal of my age group by government reports and news. I have already explained my vision is too poor for me to follow drama, but I watch news and documentaries. I am sick of the habitual representation of my group – passive, dependent, vulnerable, scroungers, a financial burden, ill, demented, a drain on the public purse, isolated, vulnerable, an escalating problem etc.

Surely I'm normal for my age – 78 – enjoying a busy life with activities and friendships. Not untypical. Ok sight loss means I receive Attendance allowance, but still pay tax so contribute, surely.

I spent the first 8 years of retirement working intensely as voluntary counsellor for an adoption organization. Work for which I'm qualified. I also served with Samaritans and as a fertility counsellor. This level of activity is absolutely typical of my generation but never mentioned in conjunction with the word *pensioner*. 'This vulnerable age-group' is the norm.

None of the dreary scenarios listed earlier apply to me or my friends. Some care devotedly for grandchildren, others work for charity, raise money, some still support parents or aged relatives, chair meetings, lead walking groups, attend classes, undertake public speaking. Many still pay tax, shop locally. A few care for chronically sick or mentally ill partners – unpaid family carers, unsung.

At least two close friends are involved in passionate affairs with younger men. This is not an aspect which gets media attention. My own love life is lively but nobody would – Who would consider putting me in a drama where the sex activities of the elderly were given anything other than comic treatment. Why not *Romeo and Juliet* in reverse? The lovers are old and it is their young, warring offspring whose objections bring them to the brink. These small samples just show how distorted are news and media representations of older people.

So why is it government/media policy to denigrate pensioners? Hidden agenda, or are the bureaucrats too sloppy to present the mixed reality?

One item that particularly irritates – the repeated advert for the advent of Digital TV. This depicts a group of old biddies gossiping about trivia, head nodding with inane grinning – intended to imply special help will be available when Digital hits their post code. What sort of damage is done by such misrepresentation?

You don't mention Radio drama which is highly thought of. Because I'm usually immersed in an audio book I don't listen to radio drama, but to many magazine and factual programmes. The one exception is *The Archers* which I've followed since Day One. They have made considerable efforts over, say, the last five years to present their old people as properly rounded characters …

I can't read newspapers or journals, but must cite one glorious exception to cardboard cut-out journalism. *The Oldie*, a journal which does what it sez on the cover – a *New Statesman/Spectator* style mag targeting older people. Edited by Richard Ingrams crammed full of literary and social comment, wit – not to be confused with *Saga* magazine. I'm fortunate to receive the journal via the Talking newspaper network. It also happens to be one of few sources of reviews of Audio books which are of course ignored by all other media.

Changed perceptions? I don't hold a limited view of my own generation so don't require enlightenment from my reading to convey their richness and variety. I much enjoyed the novel *Visitors* by Anita Bruckner whose writing throws a spotlight on the commonplace. The novel recounts the dilemmas created in the somewhat static life of an elderly widow when relatives ask her to take a young man as temporary guest in connection with a family wedding. Her experience of this unwanted presence, the light it throws on her own back-story, and the modest changes created in her obsessive life patterns are treated with the tender observation of which this author is past master. I loved it. Can you imagine that a change in an old lady's morning coffee habits could prove utterly absorbing, symbolic and deeply telling? Well it can.

Equally telling, different:- some *Talking Heads* monologues by Alan Bennett, in audio form – several, of which I particularly recall *A Cream Cracker under the Settee* with the late Thora Hird. Humour, yes, and a small amount of stereotyping, but tenderness and grief hold their own in this gem of a snapshot.

PART TWO

The Wartime Generation

6

Introducing the Wartime Generation

Of the wartime births only Joy Warren born in 1939 could even have the faintest recollection of the war, being about six when hostilities finished; of the others Doug Frendon was an infant at three, and Brenda Allen and Joanna Woods only two, in 1945. In many senses their lives are coterminous with that of the baby boomers, growing up almost entirely with the post-1945 Labour government's welfare state, as well as the gradual emphasis on youth and freedom that emerged, albeit overshadowed by the Cold War.

Reconsidering her past Joy Warren remembers certain distinct difficulties during both wartime and the subsequent years, a phase defined for her by personal deprivation and injury. She recollects her family's difficulties in sustaining life's basic requirements: 'When I was a child and my mother did not have money to buy food, she pawned her wedding ring which in those conforming and inhibiting days of the 1940s was very brave.'

For Joy this period represented a very particular upheaval and this was connected with a series of calamities for the family, although not ones defined by the physical threats usually associated with conflict, and although she suffered injury and illness, these were not directly connected to the hostilities. She details various aspects of her life, including the importance of news and a childhood accident indirectly related to the war which clearly caused her great discomfort and distress:

> We listened to the wireless a great deal – mostly the Light Programme and the Home Service. The wireless ran on an accumulator battery which was taken to a garage in the village to be re-charged.
>
> When I was three years old I was hit by an army motor biker, and spent some time in Redhill General Hospital recovering from a fractured skull and

other injuries. Parents were not allowed to visit as this was considered too upsetting to the children. When I was ready to leave I had forgotten how to walk – I don't think physiotherapy was practised then.

During this time it seems likely Joy first suffered what might be described as 'separation anxiety', a term drawing upon much earlier work by John Bowlby (who in 1939 wrote to the *British Medical Journal* warning in effect that the separation of children from parents could be potentially traumatic). Joy's first parental separation was compounded by another, for as she recalls:

> My mother became very ill with a psychiatric problem in 1944 and was in hospital for about nine months. My father took my sister and me to a children's home in Reigate. The staff could be very unkind, for example I was made to wash my soiled knickers although I was only five years old. I saw them as very big bullies and I will never forget their cruel behaviour to me. I was reading a great deal at that time having learned to read at my infant school in the village.

A further trauma followed aged seven, for when the war finished, she recalls that her father was imprisoned (which fact she only learnt about twenty years later). This event, as Joy Warren notes, was followed by certain consequences of her father's actions, for as a result of their poverty the mother and two daughters were evicted and sent to a workhouse soon afterwards:

> We went to what was still known as the workhouse. My mother needed a male sponsor to get out of the workhouse and fortunately her brother in Grimsby vouched for her and we journeyed to Grimsby in the great freeze of the winter which began January 1947.

Much later in life during the period while completing the FCMAP diaries, she reflects that from this point 'I was without a "home" until I was 30 except the homes I created in bedsits or small flats.' She also noted that 'I first doubted the existence of god when I was eight and have loathed religions all my life.' Her sense of the vicissitudes of her early life permeates her memories of many of those years. Nevertheless, after the family had been released, in the post-war period from 1947 to 1956, her recollections are detailed and relate vicariously to the conflict, particularly the conditions and experiences of those around her in her family which had been very much shaped by its traumas:

> We stayed at first with my mother's sister who was a nervous wreck from the bombing during the war. She smoked constantly, huddled by the coal fire, drinking endless cups of tea. Her husband was a fisherman and would

be away from home for many weeks. His fishing boat had been sunk at one time in the war and he survived on a raft for nearly a week before being rescued. He had to have his leg amputated which ended his work at sea.

However, throughout her life, from an early age, reading was a major and positive part of Joy Warren's experiences, offering her the foundation of later academic success, initially at school and later as an adult. She remembers such encounters fondly:

> I was entranced by Elizabeth Goudge's book *The Little White Horse* which I had for my seventh birthday. I read many Enid Blyton books and a book that one teacher led me to was *The Little Grey Men*. The Just William books were delight to me as were the Milly Molly Mandy books. By the time I was ten or eleven I was reading the Bröntes, Malcolm Saville, Kipling and then I discovered the public library stocked American crime writers such as Raymond Chandler.

Even when older she recalls her life improved greatly as she matured, concluding: 'As I have grown older I have become much happier and more relaxed. Mentally, I may not be so sharp as in my 20s and 30s but I am a lot wiser.' Unlike the generation of the pre-war births, having first in the 1960s 'gained formal qualifications which were important for my self-esteem and for a better income', Joy subsequently became what she describes as 'a middle class professional'. Equally she embraced the apparent flexibilities of freedoms of the 1970s, those rejected by the previous generation of pre-war births, changing partners frequently and the areas in London where she lived. She admits: 'I did take LSD many times in the early 1970s and had most enjoyable and enlightening experiences.' In a list in which she both summarizes and describes aspects of her varied experience through life, she notes when reviewing her early to mid-thirties under an item under the heading 'My own experience: Key changes' (which list's heading well reflects its transitions and transformations):

1970 Joined a commune in Crouch End. Communal living in a large house with members who followed exemplary careers provided good friendship for me. Married and later had my first son in 1974. Left work and commenced a period of eight years of freedom.

1975 Moved to live with my second future husband in Red Lion Square before moving south of the river and the home I still live in. Second son was born in 1976.

She also recollects the late 1970s and early 1980s after remarriage as a period of happiness, a phase whose affluence (even while she was not herself working) and stability offered an immense contrast with her childhood. She writes:

> These were very happy years and we had few money problems, took lovely holidays in France and Spain – driving and camping or staying in villas. In 1979 we bought a larger house with a huge garden in south-east London where I still live. We also bought a house in Boulogne and travelled there twice a month.

Later, on returning to work for twenty years, she gained status from running a library and the information service for a large city law firm, employing hundreds of staff, with Joy overseeing 'eight qualified assistant librarians and a secretary'. On reflection she is proud of her own professional life and that of sons, both professionals, one a museum curator and the other a photo-journalist, and pleased to be a grandmother. Curiously her mother's death liberated her, although her recollection of the events surrounding it, as prompted by the group discussion of one of the novels, indicates some sense of sadness and even guilt as to the circumstances:

> The discussions had set me thinking about my own behaviour to my mother before she died. My husband wanted her to live with us but I couldn't trust her having experienced her delusional paranoia throughout my life. She died suddenly and alone with a blood clot in her carotid artery. She suffered from blood clots because she would not take the warfarin prescribed to her as she suspected the GP of poisoning her.

Additionally she finally felt she could contact her father's relatives unrestricted by her mother's shame compounded by her other difficulties: 'I did meet some of my father's relatives after I had retired and they knew nothing of my mother's problems immediately after the war or of my father's imprisonment. Such is the secrecy within families.'

Of ageing, she notes fundamental differences, again contrasting the world of her upbringing still inhabited by certain relatives and world of the professionals in which she herself lives:

> I suppose half of the eighty-year olds I know use mobiles and computers but I don't think they are representative of most 80 year olds in this country. The retired and old people I know are from the professions and therefore more likely to use computers and mobiles. My older relatives from the agricultural labouring class use mobile phones but not computers though younger relatives are as advanced as anyone else with modern technology.

Her sense of the past allows her to savour the better life she had created for herself, the possibilities opened up by the post-war economy and welfare state, as well as the greater access to education denied her as a child, partly because of her class and her mother's occupation and dependency upon employers. She even draws upon her own past in a commune to try to imagine a better communal way of caring for (affluent) older people, with them buying in services, including nurses and servants. She judges that 'my emotions are not as easily aroused as when I was younger – thank god'. And yet something of her upbringing and past persists for as she admits of life from 2003: 'I now had freedom and became progressively happier and delighted with life. I have sufficient money to live without worrying, but continue with habits learned when young of being careful not to waste anything.'

Born in 1942, Doug Frendon was an infant during the closing years of the war. In an October 2009 directive response, he recollects aspects of his childhood:

> I was always a very 'literal' child. My birthday is on June 21st, the longest day of the year and I remember thinking that my birthday was longer than everybody else's. In the 1950 election, the headline on the front page of the *News Chronicle* the day after the General Election proclaimed:
>
> ### Labour XXX, Conservatives, XXX, Liberal 1
>
> (Obviously I can't remember the exact number of seats for the two main parties) – the point being that I knew my father had voted Liberal and I told a boy at school that that must have been his vote!

His recollection of his father (an atheist) and his mother (whom he categorizes as a non-practising Jew) is of caring and 'canny' parents despite, as he records in summer 2010, the latter being bedridden, which limited the number of friends as visitors to their home. Consequently he adapted. He remembers that 'the easiest thing to do was not to get too close to people. I can think of only three boys during my grammar school years whose homes I went to- and in each case only once. Perhaps the parents objected that I didn't return the invitation'. And possibly this was exacerbated by the conditions in the immediate post-war Britain of austerity and the uncertainties of this period.

Doug remains a private person and ruminates on his membership to a local art society after discovering a late talent for painting and drawing:

> At the first couple of meetings I went to, everybody was nice to me, but then came a lull until I was able to blend in and feel I was accepted as part of the group. This I enjoyed and put myself forward to go on the committee

and be an integral part of what was going on. But to do this properly, you have to open up and let people into your life, which I've discovered over the years is something that I want to do with only carefully selected people (who don't necessarily want to respond). So gradually my involvement with the art society waned somewhat.

He recollects that the social side of his career was limited by not having a female partner, resulting in Doug not patronizing various events, which of course also evokes the social orthodoxy of life from the post-war to the late twentieth century, which realities he admits: 'I've never really thought about it in this way before, so this is a bit of a revelation even to me.'

Earlier, aged fifty-five, winter 1997 found Doug anticipating the end of his working life in the following year: 'I'm hoping to retire in the year 2000 – like big business and all the political parties, I've developed a slogan "A new millennium, a new life" and then I expect to spend some of my time helping others, (and thus helping myself at the same time!)'.

In January 2010, Doug records the tribulations of his personal circumstances, which altered in the preceding year because of illness to his partner:

Sadly, I've had to become a full-time carer to my partner of more than 40 years – someone who used to be so strong and lively and dynamic. I don't mind in that I'm happier to have him at home rather than a care home; last year he spent more than six months between hospital and recuperation. The latter cost £1,000 a week and I eventually convinced him that I could look after him just as well at home.

Approaching his sixty-eighth birthday, by June 2010, Doug seems comfortable with both retirement and ageing, recording his daily routine. He accepts his age but grudgingly:

I'm often told I don't look my age and I certainly don't feel it, but it occurred to me this morning that if I was to be mentioned in the media for whatever reason, I would certainly be described as a 'pensioner' (true) and perhaps by some as 'elderly' (false). Heaven forfend!

His life has adapted to new technology, although in certain tasks he prefers as more traditional approach:

At ten past eight, I donned my dressing gown, checked on F [his partner, who is house-bound] and came downstairs to make a welcome cup of tea and have a quick look at my laptop. I only acquired it in January and still refer to it as 'my new toy'. I googled (should that have a capital G?) a couple of things I'd thought of during the night and then wrote my entry for yesterday in my good old-fashioned two-days-per-page diary. Much as I welcome the arrival of the computer in my home life, it will be a very long time, if ever, before I give up my handwritten diary, letters and accounts.

He reflects on the decision to end his career as an executive on a newspaper, which had been once central to his identity.

I took early retirement in June 1999, a few days after my 57th birthday, since when I've made no secret of the fact that it was one of the best things I've done in my life. In my latter years, I'd had a very stressful and demanding job and I had begun to feel it was affecting my physical and perhaps even my mental health. So, having discovered that I had a good final salary pension to look forward to, I called it a day despite advice from some colleagues that I would soon get bored. Not a bit of it, I can assure you. Certainly I hadn't envisaged the caring aspect that I've had to take on, but even so my life these days is leisurely by comparison to what came before, and I enjoy it as much as I can.

One of his weekly rituals connects Doug with his family and its past:

Tuesday is clock-winding day. We have seven in all, ranging from an art-deco style mantelpiece clock, given to my parents as a wedding present in 1939, to a longcase French one, dating from the early 1800s. Another one is the wall clock my great grandfather used to have in his grocer's shop in London's Essex Road in the 1890s, so I am the fourth generation to wind it.

And later his partner also has his lunch on a folding card table that Doug's grandparents used before the war. Again like so many people of his generation, even though only dimly aware of the conflict, the war has taken on a great significance as a landmark of change and a transformation in social mores. This too is his impression of contemporary culture, noted when he is awakened from his afternoon nap or siesta which he regards as one of the great benefits of being retired:

I was woken up by the sound of loud drilling. Next door are having some work done in the bathroom, I've discovered by following the sound. Years ago, you would always alert your neighbour if you were going to have [any] work done, but those courtesies don't seem to exist anymore unfortunately.

The same is true when pursuing a query with his bank on the telephone, when a rather young man is 'curt' and unhelpful. Doug reflects: 'I get quite cross with this modern lack of politeness and interest, and have to bite my tongue, because the only thing that suffers if I say anything is my blood pressure.'

By September 2007 Doug still records himself as single, despite having a partner, of whom there is no mention in this response. He details having both two properties with gardens (the subject of the MO directive), one in London and another in Hampshire, and describes the struggle to deal with both, given he has no great enthusiasm for gardening, although he enjoys the greenery, the bird life, which fascinates him, and the apples from his trees. He admits: 'I go to the Hampton Court Flower Show each year because I'm lucky enough to get a free ticket, but I certainly wouldn't go if I had to pay!'

By October 2009 Doug is flummoxed by the notion of thinking about Heaven and Hell but admits that at school in the late 1940s and early 1950s they were told unequivocally that there were places for the good and bad, which thought leads him to reflect upon the great numbers killed in the war. He asks his partner who replies wittily:

'I don't know, because I've never been there.' This is the same person who, when my favourite aunt died in 1985 and with whom he had had long discussions about the afterlife and whether or not it existed, had written on the card for her funeral flowers 'Now you will know the truth.'

In 1992, responding to the winter directive on 'Growing Older', Brenda Allen noted her age as '49 and three quarters!' and commented: 'I am aware of not achieving much at work, I have never married or had children; surviving to 50 (through periods of depression and difficulty) seems to me an achievement in itself.'

Here, unlike some others, there is no concern at getting older or being considered middle-aged, which is seen instead as almost a conferral of status and the opportunity for a new start. Increased longevity and the possibility of enjoying retirement, both phenomena which were widely understood by the early 1990s, were clearly having a positive effect on the general conception of ageing as a whole. Middle age is not such a daunting prospect if one is anticipating several more decades of active life.

In response to the spring 1998 directive on 'Having an Affair', Brenda notes that she has never been married but has had two affairs with married men: 'I was the "other woman"'. She goes on to say that she is 'not convinced of the need or advisability of faithful monogamy – as I was brought up to believe' and advocates a 'more generous and open attitude' to such matters. This sounds as though she has rejected the more traditional values surrounding her as a child and embraced the changes following on from the 1960s 'sexual revolution'. However, as with Beryl Saunders of the slightly older interwar generation, Brenda's attitudes are more complex and nuanced than the opening paragraphs of her directive response suggest.

As she describes her two affairs, it becomes clear that the first of these, which happened when she was twenty-eight, was very much a learning process for her. The affair, with a neighbour, lasted for three to four months but left Brenda with serious depression on and off for most of the next four years in which she remained in the same house next door to her former lover. She describes her second affair, which took place when she was forty-one, as very different. This was with a work colleague and lasted for several years. Her retrospective judgement of this affair as 'the only really serious love in my life' is very different to how she characterized her first affair. The fact that she compares herself to a bereaved wife following the end of this affair and also says that she would have liked to have married her lover under different circumstances suggests that she would have preferred a loving companionate marriage to having an affair. It was not that she was taking advantage of being single but rather that she found herself in a relationship through mutual attraction. Furthermore, she makes it clear that she never expected her lover to leave his wife – 'I could never have lived with that' – and restricts her wishes of marriage to an alternate universe in which he was not already married.

Despite her initial comments advocating a 'more generous and open attitude' to affairs, she is clearly not calling for an alternative to marriage in general and, in particular, seems rather to be promoting the idea of the companionate marriage which had become dominant in the post-war era. In fact, she is calling instead simply for more understanding of relationships that arise out of mutual attraction – a response we might equate with liberal humanism rather than a radical post-1960s take on sexual emancipation. It is significant that she ends her directive response by qualifying her original suggestion that attitudes have to change: 'I have just re-read my first comments [...] and they seem strange now that I have pointed out my experiences on paper. Writing now I would not be so hard! Perhaps I am still more mixed up than I realised.' It is as though she is feeling the pull of conflicting ideas and values and castigating herself as mixed up for acknowledging the existence of both rather than blindly adhering to one ideology over another. From the perspective of the researcher or reader, however, what comes through strongly is the capacity for self-reflective narrative, such as that promoted by MO, for representing the complex reality of cultural contestation that characterized the post-1960s decades.

We can see a similar phenomenon in Brenda's apparently conflicting opinions on the means-testing of benefits. In her response to the autumn 2006 directive on 'Age', she argues that one of the ways for governments to meet the costs of the increase in longevity would be to abolish the universal state pension and not pay pensions to those who were sufficiently wealthy or otherwise provided for to have no need of them. However, only a couple of years later at the time of the 2008 financial crisis, she was worrying about exactly such a policy of means-testing state pensions being introduced. This switch from a deliberately iconoclastic advocacy of means-testing at a time of apparent economic prosperity to a concern about it at the moment when the prospect suddenly became more real might be seen as hypocrisy or the consequence of being 'mixed-up' on these issues. However, within the context of these MO diaries, it seems more likely to be a product of self-reflective narrative's capacity to register the different competing cultural attitudes of the contemporary period. What makes Brenda's directive responses significant is not that they reveal her to be confused but that they reveal the confusion of the times. Moreover, her writing suggests that her awareness of different cultural values from the different periods of her life results not so much in an oscillation between these values but in a measured weighing up of circumstances from different perspectives. It is significant that only another year later in response to the winter 2009 directive 'Books and You', Brenda was again discussing the means-testing of benefits but perhaps in a less strident manner than in 2006, reflecting on the political barriers to addressing the manner in which 'apparently our welfare state spends more than any other in the western world on benefits for those who do not need them!' In this manner, Brenda's diary reveals a dialectical process of opinion formation.

Joanna Woods was born in 1943, an only child born into a working-class family. She writes reflexively and optimistically but includes biographical material in her diaries only sporadically.

She had neither the money nor support to pursue higher education and left her local grammar school at sixteen. Through evening study she later completed a degree in her fifties. Joanna enjoyed her work as a university administrator and was reluctant to retire. She was worried that retirement signalled the end of her 'usefulness' and that she would feel like a 'non-person' without the stimulation and social contact. Her experience has proven otherwise. She concludes: 'I have friends who I can socialize with including one or two ex-work colleagues so I do not feel isolated at all. I take advantage of concessions at the theatre etc and recently the free swimming for the over 60s.' She admits: 'I love my freedom pass which I use regularly although I must admit that I get a little miffed when the bus conductor doesn't even bother to ask me for it! Also, I have mixed feelings when a young person offers me their seat – although of course I accept gracefully.'

Joanna belongs to the WEA, socializes with friends and makes the most of concession passes to the theatre and swimming pool. She says:

I was a little reluctant to join the U3A, as I felt it was admitting I was 'old', and usually resist joining things specifically for one type of person. However, I already belong to the WEA which although a mixed aged group, has members in their 70's and 80's with razor sharp minds and I have always found older people very interesting with so much experience of life to share.

Joanna enjoys having more time to spend with her husband now that they are not working. Joanna reflects on the immense rewards of being a grandparent but feels that radically changing parenting methods create a great deal of potential for conflict and she considers the problem of 'involuntary' or enforced grandparenting:

Most grandparents enjoy 'helping out', but there are a growing number who have no choice. How fair is this? If money is not desperate, are these 'liberated women' pursuing their careers at the expense of their parents' own peaceful retirement? Young people seem to expect them to be unpaid childminders which I think is rather unfair at a time when they should be enjoying their freedom or are often looking after their own husband or wife.

Joanna was a carer for her two elderly, unmarried aunts and her mother and therefore has 'a lot of empathy with the elderly and also the conflicting emotions of a carer'. She reflects: 'The older sister had a stroke and was in a nursing home for two years, unable to speak. This was the first time that the realities of growing old really hit me. It was such a depressing place, and many of the residents had no visitors at all.' She admits that having her elderly mother live with her was a strain on her marriage. While she has two sons, one of them lives abroad, and she has no other relatives. This makes her anxious about dying alone and underpins her insistence on the importance of love and companionship in old age: 'The young do not have exclusive rights to love and happiness.'

Joanna's focus on the importance of love and companionship features in all eight of these MO and U3A diaries irrespective of the generation of the diarists. This indicates the impact of the emotional revolution over the mid-decades of the twentieth century as identified by Claire Langhamer. Viewed from this perspective, there is not a sharp divide between the attitudes of the so-called sexual liberation of the 1960s and pre-war or wartime traditional values, although it should be remembered that the diarists themselves sometimes viewed their experiences through such binary frameworks. In fact, both of these generations have negotiated the different phases of social change which have characterized the years of the welfare state by weighing up the different cultural values and attitudes of the times they have lived through against each other. Loving companionship is more important than traditional fidelity per se, but their collective sense of loving companionship embodies some of the values that were associated with traditional relationships during their early formative years.

In this respect, the two generations are not hugely different as can be seen perhaps by comparing the nuanced attitudes of Beryl Saunders and Brenda Allen, both independent women who wanted love and life on their own terms but nonetheless with a clear sense of social values. The lesser difference that emerges, however, is perhaps more significant. It is the overlapping but also slightly different values and experiences of the two generations which provide something like a stereoscopic effect, giving us a three-dimensional picture of the nuanced and complex nature of social change in the post-war years. Reading these accounts of the women diarists in particular (for a discussion of the difference between the men and the women, see the Afterword at the end of this volume) gives us a sense of how the negotiations of an ever-changing social reality, necessary to achieve agency and a sense of self, subtly altered and moved on from year to year across the period.

7

'Life Is Better Than I Could Ever Have Imagined as a Child'

Joy Warren

Joy Warren *was born in 1939 and grew up with her parents and sister in a basic farm cottage in Surrey. She had an 'erratic and disturbing' upbringing that involved a lot a family secrecy. As an agricultural worker, her father was exempt from conscription and was engaged in Home Guard duties during the war. Joy was hospitalized at three years old after she was seriously injured in an accident, and her parents were prevented from visiting her. A few years later, she was sent to a children's home while her mother was treated for a psychiatric problem. They returned to the farm cottage until her father disappeared in 1946. Joy later discovered that he was in prison. Joy and her mother were subsequently evicted and forced into a workhouse – eventually escaping to live with relatives. Joy remembers her 'utter despair' at this time, which led her to contemplate suicide. Her mother lived a transient lifestyle, so Joy attended up to twenty different schools. She eventually moved to London and lived in a women's hostel and then a communally owned house. She experimented with LSD in the 1970s and had a son in 1974. She read 'voraciously' as a form of escape and became a chartered librarian for a legal firm for twenty years, working very long hours. Her husband died in 1997. Joy feels she is 'ageing quite well'. She enjoys the greater predictability of life and feels wiser, happier and more relaxed. Since retiring in 2002–2003 she has more time for enjoyable pastimes, such as the University of the Third Age. Despite having problems with her vision, she feels she is in relatively* *good health and goes for long hikes with her philosophy group. Joy's personal experience of carers in children's homes makes her suspicious of aged care.*

As discussed in the introduction and the appendix to this book, Joy's account is taken from the autobiographical life history she wrote for FCMAP and some of the responses from her reading dairy.

I can remember sitting in a pram, laughing, about one year old with my father throwing his cap to land on my head. My mother became very ill with a psychiatric problem in 1944 and was in hospital for about nine months. My father took my sister and me to a children's home. The staff could be very unkind, for example I was made to wash my soiled knickers although I was only five years old. I saw them as very big bullies and I will never forget their cruel behaviour to me. I was reading a great deal at that time having learned to read at my infant school in the local village. At the orphanage school we learned how to divide and multiply as well as doing fractions. On VE Day we had red, white and blue ribbons tied in our hair and were each given an ice cream. Soon after that my sister and I returned to the cottage and my father planted a rose tree in the front garden. By that time I was six years old and reading the *Daily Express* or parts of it and following knitting patterns for making gloves and hats.

Disaster struck in 1946 when my father disappeared. I only learned many years later that he went to prison for petrol coupon fraud. I asked a friend whose son was a police officer to check police records and found out about the prison sentence which my mother had always kept secret. Bailiffs arrived to make us leave the cottage as it was tied to my father's job. My mother cried as she stood on the garden path which in turn caused me to cry. We went to what was still known as the workhouse. My mother needed a male sponsor to get out of the workhouse and fortunately her brother in the north vouched for her and we journeyed there in the great freeze of that winter which began January 1947.

My mother then returned to cooking which she had practised in a Lord's country home during the war. She took jobs with very wealthy families as at that time servants were difficult to find and we could stay together as a family, living in the servants' quarters. So I grew up as a child in the servants' quarters of wealthy people and my mother who was a cook was always polite and friendly towards her employers. My mother suffered from delusional paranoia which meant she moved jobs rather frequently. Apart from the usual row when she ended her jobs, she was always very positive about her work and kind to her employers. She became pregnant by one of her employers and when she moved on to another job after the birth, the little girl, my half-sister was sent to a children's home for adoption and I met her for the first time since 1948 in 2006. One family my mother worked for was outside Huddersfield. The family business was manufacturing tractors and its owner had two airplanes which in 1949 was quite unusual. I think this must have been one of the most unhappy times of my life because I remember plotting to kill myself as I felt utter despair.

My sister and I went to up to 20 schools as my mother did not stay anywhere for very long. I read voraciously – books, comics, newspapers. In Grimsby we read the *Daily Mirror* but later I would read *The Times* and whatever newspaper the employers took. During the 18 months of living in Grimsby my sister and I ran rather wild and at one point when I was eight we had a probation officer who was very kind and gave us new shoes. I didn't fall foul of the law again until I was fifteen when I almost ran down a policeman on my bicycle as I was riding at night without lights. I went to court and was fined fifteen shillings. The incident was reported in the local paper.

After moving again, amazingly I passed the Eleven Plus which I think was called the scholarship at that time. My mother still moved from job to job but managed to stay mostly in the same part of the country and I was able to remain at the same Grammar school until 1954 when she moved to another county and I went to the High School there for one term. It was during that one term that I was made to change my handwriting from looped, continuous letters to an italic style. The next job my mother took was disastrous for me, because although I was still 14, I was made to leave school and work for the same family. She moved again some months later and this time back to Buckinghamshire and I returned to the Grammar School I had attended and for some of the time as a boarder. The family my mother now worked for as a cook lived in grand style and hunted three days a week during the season. They had twelve hunters in the stables and two grooms. During the 1955 electioneering period, Anthony Eden and his wife came to stay and my mother being a strong Labour supporter managed to argue with Eden. She lost her job at about that time and it may have been because of this argument or because I was becoming reluctant to wait on their table at weekends as their parlour maid. During the school lunch breaks I saw Attlee give a speech from the back of a lorry in the poorer part of the town and later during the same campaign Churchill from the cenotaph in the town square. No senior politicians speak in public like Roman orators anymore.

A year on and after I had taken my 'O' Levels, the new family my mother was with said I could no longer stay with them as I was sixteen and should move out, so in the mid-1950s I left school. My mother and I came to London and I lived in a hostel for girls and started office work. I began to lead quite a reckless life but survived, and I read widely and was able to build on my formal education at school. After a few years and by chance I went to work in a public library and amazingly to me I was given a day off a week to obtain professional qualifications. Within four years I became a Chartered Librarian and then studied law and management at a polytechnic. Career-wise I was doing brilliantly. Every job I wanted and applied for I got, but this was as much to do with my being good-looking as for my experience and qualifications. Such is or was the world of work and selection committees comprised of men. I did make one career move in error and went to work out of London. Living as a single woman in a provincial town was not agreeable. Within a year I was back in London in a good public library system when libraries were at their peak. During the years from 1957 I read as much as possible: Homer, Herodotus, Tacitus, Suetonius, Robert Graves (Greek myths, novels and poetry); Aldous Huxley, Orwell, Hemingway, F Scott Fitzgerald, D H Lawrence, Angus Wilson and hundreds of other writers. A good guide for me was the Penguins – anything published in that series was guaranteed OK for me. I discovered middle-class, professional people through Iris Murdoch novels and by my thirties I too had become a middle class professional.

From 1970 to 1975, I joined a communal house in north London where we were all co-owners and employed our own cook and a cleaner. Members of the group were all professional people such as teachers, a doctor, a solicitor, a university lecturer. I married one of the group but our marriage only lasted two years. I was living happily in the communal house, had a very good salary, studies finished, freedom was mine and especially freedom from the bullying adults of my childhood and freedom from my mother who seemed to be relentlessly pursued by her own devils and still moving from job to job as a cook during her 50s and 60s. It was only many years later that I realized she suffered from delusional paranoia but she always managed to be one step ahead of her 'enemies' by her frequent changes of jobs.

My mother died in 1991 and was freed from her tortured life. I felt great sadness for her although at least she never seemed to be unhappy during her difficult life. I had never got in touch with my father because my mother would have considered that a betrayal. I did meet some of my father's relatives after I had retired and they knew nothing of my mother's problems immediately after the war or of my father's imprisonment. Such is the secrecy within families.

My husband died of cancer in 1997 and I continued to work for a further five years too scared to stop working and be alone. I needed to continue working to build up my pension but by the end of 2002 my worries continued over Equitable Life which held my pensions savings. The only way I could save my pension more or less intact was to retire. I now had freedom and became progressively happier and delighted with life. I have sufficient money to live without worrying, but continue with habits learned when young of being careful not to waste anything. I stopped smoking in 1999 (I did not smoke between 1974 and 1991) and I hardly drink alcohol nowadays except for some wine with dinner or at parties.

I have time to enjoy myself, seeing friends, going to the cinema, theatre, concerts, philosophy classes and the U3A reading group. This last has led me to books I would never have read alone, such as Joyce's *Ulysses*.

My disturbed and erratic upbringing could have been much worse but I learned a great deal from it and was able to have a happy marriage and bring up children who have succeeded in their own lives. I think my childhood difficulties provided a spur for me to achieve better relationships and a happy working life.

Reading was my escape as a child and later on showed me other lives. Poetry, history, philosophy is now educating me further and the more I read I realize how little I know. I am still baffled by others believing in their religions and in a god. How can people believe? I have read the Bible through and through, the Koran twice and am puzzled and alarmed by these texts. Buddhist and Hindu texts are more reasonable but again there is too much religion and as for reincarnation – one might as well believe in the Greek and Roman gods or fairies. My disbelief began when I was about eight and while I am not an out and out atheist I cannot hold any hope of there being a god. I follow the ethics of Aristotle and of Christ as written in the *New Testament* as much as possible. A C Grayling writes and speaks of philosophies of life which appeal to me.

I think I must be old but I neither feel nor behave as if I am old. I think placing people in specific categories of age depends on appearance and behaviour. Many people look a lot older than they actually are because of being overweight, ugly or unfit or badly dressed. Or, just awfully unwell and poor just like the people I often see on the streets in Lewisham. People in the City or say St James's seem to be taller and fitter than those I see locally whatever their age.

I don't know about having assumptions about people at different ages. I am interested in how they have got on; what they have achieved, how life is affecting them, their health, their habits and how much control they have over their destiny. I would now apply these thoughts to people of any age, but when I was younger I don't think I was that concerned or interested.

I do think men and women age differently. Most men don't seem to take care of themselves very well. They just don't age very well and they die at a younger age than women. They are not as sociable as women and seem not to prefer to have a life outside the home. I think I am aging quite well and am still competent in most of my activities – just hoping not to be struck down by something unforeseen. My life is fairly predictable which it certainly wasn't until I was over 25.

As I have grown older I have become much happier and more relaxed. Mentally, I may not be so sharp as in my 20s and 30s but I am a lot wiser. Physically, I am stiffening up but still swim and also regularly hike ten miles or more in the country. Stiffness means I can't easily sit in a bath so I shower instead – one is always adapting. Glaucoma came as a surprise a few years ago and my driving licence has now been renewed for three more years. My emotions are not as easily aroused as when I was younger – thank god. Spirituality – well, I experience this through music, art, prose and poetry, nature and beauty but never through religion or a god. I first doubted the existence of god when I was eight and have loathed religions all my life.

On Elizabeth Taylor's *Mrs Palfrey at the Claremont:* This could be a description of an old people's rest home rather than a comparatively expensive hotel in Kensington. Following a life as the wife of a colonial administrator, with servants and social position and now a widow, she must have found it very difficult and yet she keeps a stiff upper lip. When I worked in Kensington Public Library in the 1970s, many well-dressed, polite and charming ladies borrowed books and chatted to each other. I thought they led easy lives in their hotels. Always had company, played bridge, shopped in Derry & Toms, Pontings and Barkers. Never many men though. What a different tale is painted by Elizabeth Taylor. Well, it would be very expensive buying drinks from the hotel bar. Very sad description of Mrs Burton, the drinker – 'Mrs Burton had removed her hair-net and filled the creases of her face with powder. Her face had really gone to pieces – with pouches and dewlaps and deep ravines, as if a landslide had happened.' I should think Kensington ladies would nowadays have face-lifts and hair tinted to its colour at a younger age.

Perhaps it is the seeking of independence and inability to conform which drives the homeless onto the streets. Near where I worked in the City there was a poor old woman who would sleep in the Aldgate underpass and pulled her trolley of possessions around with her. I only saw her for a couple of years and think her hard life led to an early death. There was also an old, black woman who sat in the tunnel leading to London Bridge Underground selling the *Big Issue* for years, and now she has gone. I think the authorities tidied her away.

I still have two fountain pens and a bottle of ink but rarely use them now. Pens such as 'Uniball' are much better for handwriting than other ball-points and less bother than fountain pens. It would be foolish to throw personal papers/documents into waste paper baskets in public places. Remember the Dreyfus case and the cleaner/spy emptying the waste-paper baskets. Also, I came into my office on a Sunday and found very damaging papers had been thrown into my waste-paper basket presumably on the preceding Saturday when a member of staff had worked at my desk in its private room; the cleaners would arrive on Monday morning at 5am-ish. That was a tricky staff situation. The Blairs when at 10 Downing Street made their servants sign confidentiality agreements but Buckingham Palace staff have often managed to sell their stories to newspapers. Perhaps the Blairs were better lawyers than those employed by the Royals.

I told the group that the book [David Lodge's *Deaf Sentence*] and the discussions had set me thinking about my own behaviour to my mother before she died. My husband wanted her to live with us but I couldn't trust her having experienced her delusional paranoia throughout my life. She died suddenly and alone with a blood clot in her carotid artery. She suffered from blood clots because she would not take the warfarin prescribed to her as she suspected the GP of poisoning her.

A news item in the *Guardian* today (24 September 2009) 'Eyes on vice-chancellor over female students as "perk" remark' – suggested that female students are to be enjoyed by lecturers. Shows these professors are still at it and playing one of the games of life.

Is the technology of manufacturing hearing aids still so nineteenth century? I would have thought hearing aids would have microchips which enable them to adapt automatically to background noise without the wearer's help. Does it depend on the individual to make all the adjustments as and when required?

I know two people who are deaf and wear expensive hearing aids. One is a lawyer in his eighties who never fails to hear what I say. My lawyer friend tells me that at parties or gatherings when it is quite noisy he goes into a little haze of his own and that his hearing aids cost £6000 for a pair. And, the other, a woman of eighty who always fails to hear what one says. One gives up pretty quickly having a conversation if it means shouting. I find it easier to e-mail her than have face to face conversations. She uses an enhanced telephone when phoning me but never hears me when I phone her. Exasperating.

Muriel Spark was only 41 when *Memento Mori* was published in 1959. I first read the book when I was in my 30s and did not then appreciate how perceptive Spark was concerning all the mental and physical problems encountered by people between 70 and 90 which is the age of most of the characters in the novel. I now have much more empathy with the characters in my second reading of the book. I think MS must have known a fair number of old people and drew accurately on her observations to write this entertaining novel. She notes all their frailties – suspicions, jealousies, conniving, greed, forgetfulness, bowel and bladder problems, arthritis, deafness etc. But some of these descriptions can be applied to any age. Everyone in the reading group enjoyed this book and thought it depicted old age accurately. It is the only book we have read so far for this project which through a novel is describing the many aspects of old age and how society, wealth, poverty and health affect one's old age. The book was described as marvellous, well-written, the last word on age, a good mystery etc.

One member of my book group who has dementia says to me repeatedly that she has a perfectly good car in her garage but would I give her a lift. She may say this two or three times on the mornings I meet her but her contributions when discussing a book or event are as perceptive and intelligent as that of any other member of the group. (Her driving licence has been withdrawn by the DVLA on the prompting of her GP.)

Norah Hoult's *There Were No Windows* (concerning a scene when a servant, Kathleen, remarks unkindly concerning the dirt her mistress makes when fouling the sheets or her underwear): Well, I was about to compare this with a poem by an Irish writer which says 'Celia shits,' and, I couldn't recall the very famous writer. I knew he had written *Gulliver's Travels* and much more, was a friend of Alexander Pope, was Dean and head of a hospital in Dublin. I searched my book shelves, found the book and Jonathan Swift's poem, 'The Lady's Dressing Room.' Why could I not bring his name into my memory immediately? (On the novel as a whole): A sad and frightening story. One can only hope to have understanding and sympathetic people around one should one be similarly struck down.

General group discussion continued regarding euthanasia, Alzheimer's and living wills. Most of us thought the book to be both good and perceptive of Alzheimer's. We all recalled the frequency of going upstairs for something and forgetting the purpose of the errand. One reading group member was worried that one could be forced into suicide or euthanasia. Another reading group member admitted she has a book she bought when attending a euthanasia meeting about 40 years ago which cost £30 which tells one how to kill oneself easily. She has it hidden at home.

There was a discussion on Morden College as a refuge for the elderly and also the home that Diana Athill has recently entered. These are ideal places of last resort. Charterhouse in the City of London is also a superior refuge for the elderly. What happens to the rest who cannot get into such homes in time of need?

I think the most sensitive description in literature of a mother who is ill in bed is the one of the mother lying in bed waiting to die in *Sons and Lovers* but modern writers cannot compare with D H Lawrence. Ageing wealthy people attract relatives, servants and friends hoping to be named in a will.

I tripped on a pavement in Bloomsbury last year and the feeling I had was of shock and embarrassment and relief that a woman came immediately to help me. I only hurt my nose, surprisingly. I dislike beggars who seem to be everywhere in London. I can understand begging in India for example but not in this country. I dislike bribery, theft, domineering power and violence. I think shop assistants, officials, anyone in a public position should devote complete attention to the enquirer and not chat to colleagues, speak on their mobile and not file their nails etc. It is wiser and more attractive to keep one's upper arms covered and I am always surprised that so many men and women display their fat, floppy nakedness.

For many people who are overwhelmed by the despair and the loneliness of their lives, madness is an escape and perhaps a final refuge.

The *Guardian* and programmes on the radio provide me with details about the dreadful prospect of being in the hands of 'carers'. My own experience of 'carers' as a child in several 'children's homes' leaves me in no doubt that the ignorant bullies are still out there and inflicting their ideas and practice of 'care' on defenceless old people. As for good and bad points – I can only shrug and hope never to fall into the hands of 'carers' myself. I have no idea what older members of my family such as grandparents experienced because I have neither met nor known them. I have no experience of working in hospitals or other welfare services and I have a very low opinion of the institutional care which I read about in newspapers. My only experience is based upon my childhood incarcerations in children's homes.

I think the sort of care I might like to have would be similar to living in the household that Epicurus ran. Like-minded people would be around to discuss the arts, play cards, cook and drink wine, garden and employ servants for the heavy tasks. A modern equivalent could be for a group of friends to buy a hotel providing each member with their own room and bathroom. Communal dining, sitting rooms and gardens would provide friendly living when required and the group would employ nurses and servants as required. This would probably depend on the financial ability of people to buy and sell shares in the property or something like a housing association could be formed.

As for what care for older people will look like in the next 10–15 years? This will depend upon the economics and the wealth of the country. With this country's enormous debt and fewer people in employment providing less money through taxation it is unlikely that extra funds will be directed to the care of old people.

I think political correctness nowadays makes officialdom more respectful towards older people today. One observes a great deal of kindness by individuals towards older people but, respect – no.

Anyway, if what James Lovelock and George Monbiot as well as others are predicting comes true, it is not the older generations who will be in trouble – it will be our children and grandchildren. The well-off will be able to secure and buy their safety from the ravages of global climate change and the rest could be surviving in very primitive conditions.

My favourite age? Well, I have liked whatever age I have been. And, life is immeasurably better than I could ever have imagined as a child. The only thing I might have done differently would be to have started studying earlier but I had no support or encouragement. And, more significantly, no family.

8

'An Apprentice Old Dear'

Doug Frendon

Doug Frendon was born in 1942. He lives in London, has a second home in Hampshire and owns a flat in Spain. Before volunteering to retire early, Doug worked as a promotions manager for a national newspaper. Doug was born in the middle of the Second World War and has no early memories of it, although he remains sensitive to the sound of approaching aircraft. His mother died suddenly and shockingly at the age of fifty-three in a care home. He was heavily involved in caring for his father and stepmother when they slipped into dependency, which he found very difficult. He relates this period to his subsequent struggle with depression. Doug now has very little contact with his own family but has an 'adopted' Catalan family through his long-term (male) partner, who he lives with and acts as a carer for.

After retiring, Doug discovered his artistic talents and joined a local art society. He finds it easier to talk to people as an older man and has been involved in various kinds of volunteer work (including work at the Mass-Observation Archive and the London Transport Museum). He suspects that others see him as 'a bit of a loner' but considers himself 'an affable sort of chap, well liked and trusted by those that know me, and a reliable and constant friend to the few I "allow" to be part of my circle'. The faster pace of life in London often makes him feel impatient, though he has learnt not to 'clock watch' now that he is 'past the stage of wanting to rush'. When the recession hit he took 'perverse delight' in blaming Gordon Brown. He was not seriously concerned with his ability to live comfortably as he owns shares and property.

Aside from the three main directives discussed in the introduction and appendix of this book, the material in this chapter is also taken from replies to the following MO directives: 1992 'The Pace of Life', 1994 'Death and

Bereavement', 2001 'Media and the Public Interest', 2009 'Mid-life Transitions', 2012 'The "Big Society"', and 2012 'Photos, Music and Memory'.

Spring 1992, aged 49: In London I tend to walk quite quickly and get impatient when people get in my way on crowded pavements. [...] In general, I think I have adapted my pace of life to just about the right level. On Mondays to Fridays I have a fairly well-balanced routine which, although hectic at times in business hours is comparatively relaxed. [...] At weekends too I try not to cram too much into the time available and, if this means that I don't go out socializing as much as I used to, well – this might be a sign of age – but so what? I really have passed the stage of wanting to rush here and there, cramming in as much as possible into the shortest amount of time.

However, it hasn't always been thus. For about four or five years leading up to my father's death in November 1990 I had to make frequent and sometimes unscheduled visits to see him and my stepmother (who died in September 1989). Both were in their eighties when they went and both had struggled to maintain their independence and stay in their own home. But of course there were all sorts of things to do on their behalf and my weekends had to revolve to a certain extent to at least one visit to them (fortunately they lived only about a 20 minute drive away). In 1986 my partner and I bought a second home, so since then there have been four lots of grass to cut (2 in London [front and back] and 2 in Hampshire), two houses to keep clean and so on. For a time, the pressures got to me and I suffered what I suppose is called 'depression' for about a year. The one good thing to come out of that has been the realization that, whatever problems I face now (and they really are few) I can cope with them all and so I don't get worked up.

1992, aged 50: I have just written at the side of this sheet that I am 50. I have been this age for six months now but it still surprises me when I have to write it down or hear myself saying it. In fact, I have got to the stage where I don't voluntarily admit my age.

People tell me that I look about 40 and I suppose that is about the age I feel. When I had my 40th birthday, it left me unmoved, but when I reached 45, it hit me fairly hard. Admittedly, there were a few factors that probably contributed to this – deaths in the family, burst pipes at home, aged parents to worry about – and I was depressed (which is unusual for me) for over a year.

There are adverts around these days for people of fifty and over – to join clubs. To get reduced car insurance, to go on special holidays – and it suddenly hits me that this includes me! I suppose at 50 I must be considered middle-aged, although I would hate to admit it to anyone.

Without wanting to sound mercenary, being comfortably off has, to me, been one of the benefits of growing older. Other gains include being able to deal with difficult situations and difficult people more easily and with less embarrassment, and a greater awareness of how not to tread on other people's toes.

Now that I am 50, I am conscious that I may well retire in the next ten years. In our company you can retire on full pension nowadays at 62. The pension scheme is such that an old hand like me who has been paying in for many years (and into a supplementary fund too for extra benefits) could retire on a reasonable pension at age 55 say, always assuming that inflation doesn't inflate too dramatically again.

I am very conscious that the hobbies and interests one has now and squeezes in at weekends or spends more time on at holiday periods would be hard pressed to fill all the time one has after retirement. So I think I would want to do some voluntary work on one or two days a week. I also want to take piano lessons again and perhaps even buy a piano. I know I'm never going to be very good at my age but I can amuse myself happily for an hour or two at the keyboard – as long as nobody else is listening!

As I've said earlier, we have a flat in Spain – in Barcelona, in fact, where my partner has relations. It would be nice to spend two or three months at a time there and I vaguely wonder if we could settle there. When I was a child, I always wanted to be a teacher. This wasn't to be but, if we did settle abroad, I would certainly want to try my hand at giving English lessons.

Spring 1994, aged 51: The first person I remember 'dying' was my mother's Auntie Pauline, who died in 1950 when I was 8. She used to come and see us sometimes and we always had to be on our best behaviour because she appeared to me a stern old lady. I had embarrassed my mother once by asking Auntie Pauline when she was born – but she was greatly interested in the answer – 1881 – because nobody in the family had ever known!

I don't remember being affected in any way, nor when her husband, Uncle Isaac, died three years later except that there were two small causes of excitement here – one, in that my brother and I were each due to inherit £45 from his will and, secondly, I was the one who answered the phone when cousin Alfred phoned to tell us the sad news.

Whilst preparing some notes for this piece, I suddenly remembered that when I was 12 or 13, the District Commissioner of our Boy Scouts in Finsbury, London, died suddenly leaving two children of about my age. It was just before Christmas and although I didn't feel sad for him, I was moved about the children without their father at what should have been a happy time.

Obviously I must have heard of deaths in the succeeding years but nothing was to prepare me for the fateful happening on August 12th (the Glorious Twelfth!) 1961 when my dear mother died suddenly and unexpectedly.

I must sketch in some background here. We lived 'over the shop' which my father ran, while simultaneously caring for my mother who had been completely bed-ridden for 12 years. He had also brought up two boys and we were now 21 (my brother) and 19. Because of the strain on my father, 1961 was the second or third year when my mother had gone into hospital for a fortnight to give him a break physically. Although we visited regularly, it wasn't a happy time for any of us, least of all my mother because St Matthews Hospital in Shepherdess Walk was an old workhouse and had been turned into a geriatric hospital with vast wards. She was only 53 but there was nowhere else she could go.

August 12th was a Saturday and she was due to come home on the Monday. My brother had gone off that very morning on a cycling holiday to Yugoslavia and at 7 p.m. I was dressing myself up to go to the West End. I then realized that my wallet was missing and my father and I were discussing whether one of the lodgers could have pinched it when the telephone rang. I answered it.

'This is St. Matthew's Hospital. Mrs [word is scored out] is seriously ill and can be visited at any time.' (So clearly do I remember the matter-of-fact tone of voice of the man and his exact words that I wrote my mother's surname just then without thinking of your anonymity requirements).

Dad and I set off immediately. It was one of those awkward journeys that could be quicker by bus if one came along but generally quicker on foot through the back streets. I was surprised to think that somebody could become seriously ill so quickly (I had visited the night before) and I was genuinely shocked when my father suddenly said as we were walking, 'What happens if she's dead?' In retrospect after 33 years with much experience of euphemisms and the way of the world, I can see why he thought that but at the time I was young and naïve.

We arrived at the hospital. It was really old-fashioned even then and once my father had told the gate porter who we were, we had to wait just inside the main gate with nowhere to sit (and no room anyway) with white painted staircases up and down to right and left of the porter's cubby hole.

It was here that the doctor came to us and told us with no preamble that my mother had died in the last few minutes. I think we both cried there and then despite people going past. The shock was tremendous. They asked my father if he wanted to see my mother. We were taken to this vast ward. All the old people were already tucked up in bed for the night, despite daylight through the windows. Some were rambling in their minds, one was shouting. My mother's bed was screened off of course. When they took us through the curtains, there was my dear, dear mother almost sitting up in bed (when she was at home she was always on her back with just her head raised) with a bandage tied round her head from top to bottom (I found out afterwards to keep the jaw shut). I just turned round and almost ran out of the ward in my distress. Some of the old dears realized what was happening and made sympathetic noises. Nothing could have prepared me for the terrible, terrible shock of the evening's events (it must have been less than an hour from the phone call to that point) and I can almost feel tears at the back of my eyes as I write of these happenings nearly 33 years later.

Such was my first experience of grief, not only in myself but seeing it in other people and, of course, my father and I reacted in different ways.

At 19, I had my life in front of me. I missed my mother dreadfully. Because she was bedridden, she had always been there when I got home from school. She had helped me with my homework, we used to do the shop accounts together, I used to write letters at her dictation. I used to read bits out of the paper to her when her eyesight got bad and would give a running commentary when we were watching TV plays (so-and-so has gone out of the room, somebody else has just come in, and so on).

Her bed was the main focal point of our sitting-room and now it was empty. After all these years I can still vividly remember a dream I had a few days later in which I was standing at the front of her bed saying to her 'Oh, so you are alive after all.' When I woke up and realized it was only a dream I cried.

Her funeral was the first I had ever been to. We followed the hearse the eight or nine miles to the crematorium at Streatham (it was one of the nearest to us and it was where my father's father had been cremated) and I remember that from my seat in the funeral car I had a clear view of the coffin. There were eight or nine people there. I broke down during the service and my father and I sobbed in each other's arms. Now there *are* tears in my eyes as I write. As you can imagine, no other death has affected me so strongly since and, as I get older, I suppose no other death will in the future, even that of my partner if I am the survivor.

I hope I don't sound unfeeling, but within a week or two I remember buying a bright blue shirt (still not very common in 1961) and gramophone records. I went back to work after the funeral and my life, despite the great sadness I felt, soon resumed a degree of normality.

Not so for my father. For a man of 57 to lose his wife, the mother of his two children, and somebody whom he cared for emotionally and, in this case, physically too (to the extent of treating bed sores, changing soiled bed sheets and so on), the loss must have been staggering. The shop had been losing money for years and was only clinging on by the financial contributions my brother and I were making now that we were at work. Dad's reason for living had gone and, had he been a different kind of man, I think he might have taken his own life to follow my mother.

As it was, he didn't want to wash or shave or change his clothes. He felt guilty for all the times he had shouted at my mother (he had a quick temper) and for all the things he could have done but hadn't. I kept telling him that nobody could have done more than he had but he told me I didn't understand which I'm sure I didn't. For instance, I was listening to the radio 3 or 4 weeks later and was joining in with a Connie Francis song that was popular at the time that had the words 'we strolled the lanes together, sang those refrains together, etc. etc.' I was quite upset that he shouted at me to switch it off and then burst into tears. I thought that by then he should have 'got over it.'

Afterwards, he was to say that it was only me being there that had got him through those first few lonely weeks. At Dad's request my brother had continued his holiday in Yugoslavia (which can't have been a bundle of fun in the circumstances). He and my father had not in recent years been close like Dad and I had, and I don't think they were able to offer each other a lot of comfort when my brother arrived home. Anyway, within two months, he had his first overseas posting with his job, and it certainly eased the tension when he went away.

This response about death and murder made me also think of Rachel Nickell. She was the attractive young mother who was stabbed to death on Wimbledon Common in front of her three-year-old son, who was found shortly afterwards clinging to her body and imploring her to 'get up, mummy.'

The common is within walking distance of my home and I often used to go there with the dog (who has since died). Being a middle-aged man, I didn't feel in any way that I could be in danger but, because of what had happened and the terrible and brutal manner in which it was done, I avoided that part of the Common where the murder occurred. Then I discovered a few weeks later that the scene of the crime was elsewhere to what I had thought and that, in avoiding what I had thought to be the place, I had actually walked past several times where the poor girl had been killed. I was very unhappy about this and felt that, in going past the spot, I had somehow invaded the privacy and grief of her death – so I stopped going to that area of the Common at all.

On reflection I am surprised at the strength of my own emotions when I was writing about the death of my mother back in 1961, over 30 years ago.

Autumn 2001, aged 59: Since I retired in 1999, I have much less contact with other people – I'll rarely discuss anything in the news with the friends, relations and other people I meet, and the organizations to which I belong are not news-based in any way.

Autumn 2006, aged 64: [despite the directive being issued in 2006, response dated 23 March 2007]: N.B. I responded to this directive in 1992 when the title was Growing Older. I wrote 10 pages. Let's see what happens this time.

In June [2007] I shall reach my 65th birthday, and writing that down just now gave me a slight jolt. Of course I've had plenty of notice of its impending arrival – through my earlier life there were two special years I was aiming for: 2000 for obvious reasons, and 2007 for my retirement.

In fact, I took early retirement in 1999 after 35 years with the same company, and I am happy to say that life is rosy. I'm settled, solvent and healthy and I was delighted to be told a couple of years ago that I looked 47, which is about the age that I feel now. That would make me middle-aged and, years ago, I would have said that 65 was approaching elderly. … But there's no way that I would use those two words to describe myself today. Since my

60th birthday when I become eligible for 'concessions' at theatres, galleries etc., I've described myself jokingly as an 'apprentice old dear', becoming a 'fully-fledged old dear' in June next. It's hard to face the truth sometimes!

I've long had the vague idea that I'm going to live to be 84, so I've got twenty years to go. In some ways I can accept that and, for example, when they talk on the radio or in the press about forecasts for, say 2030, I realize that I may well not be here. A few years ago that would have depressed me, but now I can accept it more easily. Perhaps my only sadness (if you can call it that) is that I won't be around perhaps when the children of friends and my nieces grow into mature adults and have families of their own. On the other hand, with all the talk of water shortages, flooding and other effects of global warming that could be imminent I'll be better off out of it (especially as I might not be able to cope if I become aged and infirm as happened to my father). He had been so strong in character, temperament and fortitude (and he had had some big problems to deal with during his life) that it was especially sad to see him fade away and become dependent on others by the time he died at the age of 86.

The third [key change in my life] happened in 1999 when I volunteered for early retirement. The pressures on the previous few years at work had been enormous and I was finding the changeover to computer technology difficult to get on with. I'd always been a meticulous person and was well-known for my attention to detail and to an extent I felt I was losing control. I'd been working long hours and was losing confidence in myself so having discovered that because of my long service and a very good pension scheme I would be able to live comfortably in retirement (even allowing for inflation). I decided to retire. My mantra to the many colleagues who expressed astonishment at my early departure was 'a new century a new life'. I should add that I invariably showed a sunny disposition to outsiders and many considered me to be a workaholic wondering how I would cope with retirement.

I knew of my inner fear, the panic attacks, the feeling that my heart was racing at times, and I was beginning to worry about my long-term health. I knew that I would cope well with retirement, and my confidence has been justified. On the rare occasions I'm invited back to the office (like that retirement party I mentioned earlier), everyone tells me how well I look and how relaxed I seem … which I truly am.

Any problems I have these days are trivial by comparison to those in my work towards the end, and I know that they'll sort themselves out in time or I will be able to overcome them. That's one of the advantages that has come with age.

Another is that, contrary to what happens to some people I am becoming less pedantic. This is no bad thing, because there was a time, say ten or twelve years ago, when I was aware myself that I was becoming too fussy. Thinking of it now (having just re-read what I've already written here), it could have been my way of fighting that feeling of losing control. Nowadays, if I find that something is not where it should be or hasn't been done by the time that it should, it might be a nuisance – but it's not the end of the world and hopefully not worth getting steamed up about.

Winter 2009, aged 66: What has surprised most people, I am sure, is the speed at which the 'credit crunch' has enveloped our lives, and also the global extent of it.

I took some perverse delight in 'blaming' Gordon Brown for it all, a man I've never liked or trusted, and, in this context, I mention a conversation I had with a Spanish friend in Barcelona, where I arrived on the very day when Tony Blair made his (sob, gulp) resignation announcement. I was asked if I was sorry to see him go. My answer was 'good riddance' followed by 'But you ain't seen nothing yet. Just wait until Gordon Brown becomes P.M.' My host was very surprised at my reaction, but has commented since that my forecast was an accurate one. I'm sure that neither of us at that time (May 2000) had any idea how both our countries' economies were going to be affected.

As for my own situation, I consider myself very fortunate. I have no mortgage or debts to worry about. I receive the government pension, and a generous one from my former employer for whom I had worked continuously for 35 years, paying the maximum pension contribution possible for many years. Life for my parents had always been a struggle (the thirties, the Second World War and severe health problems for my mother from the mid-40s until her death in 1961) and they were keen, equally as I was eager, that I should have a better lifestyle than theirs (which is why my first job on leaving school was with the Westminster Bank, a well-respected company with an all-important pension scheme). I've always been 'prudent' with money (and as a child we had to be and old habits die hard) and I've used that word since long before G Brown introduced it into his lexicon. Of course it occurs to me that my pension fund must have been badly hit by the current downturns, but they've always assured us that it is extremely well-funded, and indeed, the parent company is one of the few in its field to still operate a final salary pension scheme. So I'm keeping my fingers crossed.

Of course, though interest rates on savings have plummeted, I'm happy (although I can assure you not smug) enough to say that 'I'm short of a few bob' and I'll survive comfortably. Where I have lost out is on shares. I always tot up the value of my portfolio every six months. In February 2007 it was £29,000, in August 2008 £14,000, October 2008 £10,000 and now [January 2009] £8,500. Most of my shares came from privatization issues so I didn't buy them and so technically I haven't lost anything. Similarly with property. However much I get when I sell (or my estate sells) will be many tens of thousands of pounds more than I paid years ago. Because by necessity I've become a carer to a very old friend, I 'go out' very little, but when I do visit a gallery, say, I'm often shocked by the prices, and still, from habit, visit the cheaper restaurants when I meet a friend for lunch. How families manage I don't know and there's a lot to be said for the position I find myself in now (financially).

Winter 2009, aged 67: As a child, I read avidly and was encouraged to do so, especially by mother. The *News Chronicle* (sometimes just four pages in the early years after the war), one or two comics a week and books from the Finsbury Public Library, an imposing Victorian building where silence was the norm and where I felt privileged (in an area where many adults, let alone their offspring, struggled to read) to be able to bring home two or three books of my choice.

This became a contentious issue when I reached 10 or 11, because my mother said ... I should be bringing home The Classics. Well-intentioned aunts and uncles would give me titles like *Kidnapped* or *Treasure Island*, which didn't appeal to me at the time and, which, I've never read since. Suddenly though something clicked and I began to devour Arnold Bennett, W.W. Jacobs, Norman Collins, H.E. Bates and even a touch of Dickens ...

Paradoxically, I've always belonged to a public library until I retired, because train journeys to and from the office were an ideal time to read (sometimes I even welcomed a delay so as to be able to finish a chapter or get through a few more pages).

Since retirement ten years ago, I've maintained my membership with the local library but use it very rarely. With the changing pattern of life and of my life, I don't seem to want to make time to read books and, on the rare occasions I do, I've plenty of unread tomes on my own bookshops to choose from.

Deep down, I like novels where there is a satisfactory, but not necessarily happy, ending (such an example is Daphne du Maurier's *Rebecca*, which had me on the edge of my seat to the very last page). At school, I became good at writing essays (a useful trait at being a good Mass Observer I always feel) and I well remember being taught at junior school in the early 50s, the positive need for 'a beginning, a middle and an end.' Sounds sensible, but so often not apparent in other peoples' writings.

I was recently asked if I intended to join a local book group, but I declined. Even the member who asked me said she found it impossible sometimes to work up any enthusiasm for a book that didn't appeal to her and, although she is certainly not lacking in personality or confidence, to then offer some positive contribution to the general debate.

Winter 2009, aged 67: I don't think I've come across the phrase 'mid-life transition' before and had to stop and think if I'd had one! Being 67 now, obviously I did and I presume you mean that period of life when one enters one's forties, or thereabouts. For me, this transition was no more or no less important than entering any other decade of my adult life. However, if you ask if I had a mid-life crisis, the answer would definitely be yes, and I've written about it before for Mass Observation.

It started in the spring of 1987 when I was 44. During the previous winter my favourite aunt had died unexpectedly aged 71. Ten weeks later, her older sister died just before her 77th birthday. These were my mother's sisters (my mother had died unexpectedly in 1961 aged 53). My father and stepmother, both in their 80s, were finding life more and more difficult, and I had to make regular visits to keep an eye on them and lend a helping hand. On top of all this, we'd bought a second home in the summer of 1986 (fortunately only an hour's drive away in Hampshire). We'd been for the weekend and intended to come back to London on the Sunday afternoon, January 11th 1987 but heavy snow started falling about 10 a.m. and we beat a hasty retreat, so hasty that we forgot to leave the central heating on. The second aunt mentioned above died that evening and because of her funeral etc. and also bad weather, it was a fortnight before we could go back. On arrival we found water dripping through the ceiling from 11 burst pipes! I've always been quite good at responding to a crisis and in the short term I performed well. But I suppose accumulation of events coupled with the realization that I was probably more than half-way through my life (for many years I was certain I was going to die when I'm 84, but as this age gets nearer I'm hedging my bets!), I entered a period of what I now realize was a mild depression.

Because I'm a cheerful and confident person to the outside world, few people ever bothered to find out if I was different inside – but I was. In 1983 I'd had a panic attack during a particularly stressful period at the office, and I now had to fight the resurgence of such feelings. I had good days and bad days and my inner confidence could vanish in an instant. I still remember vividly driving home from work one Friday evening. We had plans for the weekend and I was feeling happy and relieved to be so. I had to wait at traffic lights under the railway bridge in Blackfriars Road, London and suddenly the gloom descended. It was awful and I could have cried on the spot. The whole 'depression' lasted about a year and, despite difficult periods in my life during the last 20+ years, I'm happy to say that I've coped with everything that's come along. Today is 1st January 2010 and I'm reasonably optimistic about the year ahead, despite having to be a full-time carer to my partner of more than 40 years.

Spring 2012, aged 69: I seem to remember David Cameron having big plans, possibly about a year ago and about ten months into his prime ministership, for what he called the Big Society. It was all about thinking of ways of helping other people, principally by doing voluntary work, doing one's bit for the local community and for neighbours, and generally being much less selfish than the way the nation seems to have become. It didn't seem a particularly new idea, although I can't pinpoint an exact time when I had heard such suggestions before.

I took early retirement almost thirteen years ago and undertook voluntary work from the word 'go.' For a year and a half, I used to drive down once a fortnight to the University of Sussex and work in the offices of the Mas Observation Archive, for whom I had been writing since 1986. I'd written to Dorothy Sheridan saying I would like to help and she wrote back immediately and said 'yes please.' At first I found the pace of office life there very slow (after working 35 years in a major company rushing hither and thither and getting stressed out in the last 5 years of my career); also I had to come to terms with the fact that I was just a volunteer helper and I wasn't expected to try and organize things or take decisions as had become my custom by necessity.

After that I passed the driving test of the Institute of Advanced Motoring (something I had wanted to do for years but had never had the time) and, at their suggestion became an Observer, i.e. taking people out for an hour on a Sunday morning and advise on ways they could improve their motoring skills. I enjoyed this very much but I was having back problems at the time and found that getting in and out of other people's cars on damp winter mornings and (sometimes if they weren't very proficient) living on one's nerves for an hour not conducive to my health, so I reluctantly had to give it up after a couple of years. Simultaneously I went once a fortnight to do voluntary work for the London Transport Museum. I have been interested in London's various forms of transport since I was a small boy and it was fascinating working behind the scenes and finding out even more than I already knew about the history of the capital's buses, trams, trains etc. The museum was very grateful for the work carried out by volunteers and laid on a Christmas party for them each year, but on an individual basis I found some of the staff tended to ignore us or give us jobs they didn't want to do themselves.

These days, I'm a full-time carer for my partner which I suppose is called voluntary work, because I don't (and nor do I expect) to be paid for so doing. Although I am able to go out for up to four hours at a time, I can't commit myself to any other outside voluntary work because his needs can vary from day to day, even sometimes from hour to hour.

Spring 2012, aged 69: I was born in 1942 at the now long gone St James's Hospital on the edge of Wandsworth Common in south London. Since then I have lived at ten different addresses (my present one for the last forty years) and all of them have been in the London Postal area.

There is no song that reminds me of childhood – my father had been a keen theatregoer before the war, especially to musicals, and was always singing extracts from various numbers. Trouble was though that he usually only seemed to know only the first few lines after which his singing would fade away or he would make up his own words (usually comic and he was quite good at it). My mother preferred classical music and would occasionally listen to concerts on the Third Programme (as Radio 3 was called then), but as the only radio was in our main living room she didn't get much chance.

The first record I bought was in September 1958 just after I'd started work. It was an instrumental piece called Hushabye (on the B side was Whistlin' Rufus) and it had been the signature tune of a radio serial at that time. From what I remember the serial was either a thriller or a murder case – I recall I lost interest by about episode three or four but I liked the signature tune so much that I would switch it on just so as to hear the music. I've just been upstairs to look for the record to check who it was by (I think it was Monty Sunshine), but I haven't played it for years and it wasn't where I expected it to be, but I did come across a whole box of other 45s I bought in the late 50s and throughout the 60s – and boy, have I got a lot of listening and reminiscing to do! Tunes from that time can be so evocative … who was I in love with or perhaps who was I infatuated with at the time for example. Singers include Cilla Black (my favourite), Frank Ifield, Del Shannon, Helen Shapiro, John Leyton and a whole lot more. Numbers with special significance include 'Moon River' (Danny Williams), 'I Love You Because' (Jim Reeves) and 'Those Were The Days' (Mary Hopkin).

Music plays an important part in my life. Sadly I never learnt to play an instrument, although I started on the piano aged about 12 but some of the notes didn't work and it badly needed tuning, two good excuses at the time for not practicing! I have a large collection of LPs, 45s, some of my father's pre-war 78s, cassettes and to a lesser degree CDs. I have what is called catholic taste from opera to Cliff Richard and from a large gathering of zarzuelas (comic operas) from Spain to sound tracks from films and shows.

When I go to bed at night I put Classic FM on the sleep facility for 30 minutes and I rarely notice that the music has stopped.

Moving on photographs – when my father died in 1990 I 'inherited' his large collection of family photos going back to the early 1900s (there is one picture of him in dresses when he was just a few months old in 1905, with his parents, his maternal grandparents and one set of maternal great-grandparents!). As I'm a person who instinctively collects things, I also have a large collection of my own photos. They are in various boxes and folders around the hose and I always mean to catalogue them but never do. I'm now approaching 70 and wonder what to do with all these memories. I have nephews and nieces who seem to have little interest in their ancestors but I find it physically difficult to throw away (I certainly couldn't tear up) photos of people I've known and sometimes loved. At odd times during my life I've possessed a camera but never with great enthusiasm. So often there was that disappointment when collecting developed photos from the chemist, having waited impatiently for them to be ready, and seeing the results were nowhere nearly as good as I had hoped.

We have a few framed photographs around the house, my favourite being a small black and white snap taken in 1947 on Margate promenade during the only family holiday we ever had (two years later my mother became bedridden). It is also the only photo that exists of my mother, father, brother and me all together. It measures just 3½ by 2½ inches and shows my elder brother and I sitting on a stuffed lion with my father at one side and my mother on the other. I think we went in June and the weather must have been quite good because we boys are just in shirts, shorts and sandals (no socks and the shirts were long-sleeved). My father though was wearing a suit and a tie, my mother was wearing an overcoat. My brother, father and I were all smiling – my mother, who didn't like to have her photo taken, was clearly wanting it to be over and done with. Although I've looked at this photo thousands of times, I've now just noticed that the stripes of my father's tie go diagonally from right to left, suggesting it came from the U.S.A. I'm sure he can't have known because he hated all things American, but I suppose in those days you would wear whatever you could lay your hands on that looked smart. Another framed photo shows my brother and me in our back garden in Streatham – in his left hand my elder brother is holding a Union Jack, the other hand is holding one of mine. The year was 1945.

On display also we have a colour photo I took in 1988 of my partner's mother with her first great-grandchild, a b+w2 studio shot of my father in a suit and looking rather serious taken during the war, a studio photo of my mother aged 10 in 1918 with her three younger siblings, a colour snap of a lovely German Shepherd dog we had for eight years, and two pics taken during my time in the late 70s running a Christmas charity for sick children – in one I'm showing a gigantic teddy bear to Princess Anne (for some reason the photographer wanted her to touch it but despite my best efforts she didn't). In the other I'm introducing Mrs Thatcher (then Leader of the Opposition) to a member of my staff.

I haven't learnt yet to download photos on to my computer, but my mobile phone screensaver features one of my own paintings, of four Catalans dancing La Sardana (their national dance). I don't share my music or photographs with anyone. Technically I don't know how to and physically I wouldn't want to for fear of not getting them back.

Another photo is upstairs somewhere and was taken by my father in 1968 when my partner and I were in the early stages of our relationship and I was 25 and he was 41. It was a very muzzy black and white snap, taken by my father near his caravan on the Isle of Sheppey and we are playing miniature golf. It must have been a hot day because we are both stripped to the waist but we look younger than our years and we both look very happy.

I have pictures of London streets taken in the late 40s [and] early 50s when I was growing up. I love street scenes where you can see the shops and what's in their windows, the fashions of the time worn by the passers-by, the lamp posts and other street furniture, but most importantly public transport-trams, motor buses and trolleybuses. Some photos, and I must have hundreds of them in the many, many books I have on the subject, show an incredible amount of detail (especially if you use a magnifying glass) like adverts on hoardings and the sides of buses and trams plus their numbers and destination blinds/boards. Every picture tells a story they say and in some photos you can almost hear the ambient noises but also notice the lack of private cars and very few traffic lights even at major junctions.

9

'Politicians Need to Chat Up the Older Generation'

Brenda Allen

Brenda Allen *was born in 1943. She is single with no children and lives in Chesterfield, Derbyshire. She retired early from her job as an auditor at the age of fifty-four, claiming it 'saved [her] sanity'. Brenda reflects on how working environments have transformed since she began working in 1963. Despite improvements, she has 'no desire to work for anyone again. I am not giving up my independence'. Brenda has been involved in two serious affairs with married men. She describes her experiences of being the 'other woman' in detail and critically reflects on monogamy and marriage. She thinks that older women seem younger these days, as they are more active, have 'greater freedom of self-expression' and 'no longer need to conform to stereotypes'. 'I have noticed myself as I have got older that I am now more socially acceptable than I was before', she writes: 'Women who in the past would have ignored a single woman such as myself now realise that they have to mix with us.' Brenda identifies with the post-war generation as opposed to older pensioners and ponders the consequences of means-testing for state pensions and benefits. When her frail, elderly mother was in a nursing home, Brenda felt obliged to stay in contact with her. She has a tense and competitive relationship with her siblings; their mutual sense of duty to their mother is the only 'link' that keeps them in contact. 'We are a jolly lot aren't we?' she writes of her family: 'Although [we're] aware of the tensions, and feeling sore, we all keep up appearances.'*

Aside from the three main directives discussed in the introduction and appendix of this book, the material in this chapter is also taken from replies to the following MO directives: 1998 'Having an Affair', 2000 'Gays and the Family', 2008 'World Financial Crisis' and 2009 'Mid-life Transitions'.

Winter 1992, aged 49: Getting to this age seems quite an achievement, it feels like a notable event. But it also makes me aware of the passing years. I shall have to admit to being middle-aged but I feel that gives me a bit of status – perhaps because there is nothing else in my life that gives me that feeling. I am aware of not achieving much at work, I have never married or had children; surviving to 50 (through periods of depression and difficulty) seems to me an achievement in itself.

It also feels like a new start – start of what I don't know, but somehow it's a turning point. I am trying to think of a way of marking the occasion. It has affected me in one way – I am refurbishing the lounge, getting rid of my 1970s soft furnishings and replacing with more up to date stuff (again a fresh start, a new beginning).

Reading the above shows I have a positive attitude to getting older, I suppose like most people I see 'old' as older than I am now. When I was young old was probably 50–60, but now I realize that old = at least 80!!

At nearly 50 the menopause will hit me soon, no doubt. I feel fine at the moment but physically I have started to look older in the last year or two. I am growing grey, sagging a bit, but not putting on weight except when I give in to the chocolates, and my face and neck are 'loosening'. I have even vaguely wondered about a face lift then dismissed the idea as vanity.

Women make more effort to look and act younger, but surely this is in reality an act of running away from getting older. If it really was OK to be older they would let the years take their physical toll without any cosmetic aids. Women like actresses Jane Collins or Jane Fonda do not make it OK to be 50-something, only to be 50-something and looking only 40. No way is this an acceptance of getting older.

Spring 1998, aged 54: I have not been married myself – the only 2 serious affairs I have had have been with married men, so I was the 'other woman'. I have not been the wronged wife, so I cannot comment on how that would feel. Perhaps that makes my views and feelings rather selfish?

My views on marriage and faithfulness cannot be those of a married person; no doubt I would feel differently if I had seen this issue from the opposite perspective. I am not (now I am older (middle-aged) and wiser) convinced of the need or advisability of faithful monogamy – as I was brought up to believe. Perhaps much of the angst of partners discovering affairs comes from this rather old-fashioned idea, and from an unrealistic expectation of faithfulness. A more generous and open attitude could remove much unnecessary guilt.

I am not aware of my brothers or sister having affairs, nor my parents. However they would not confide in me, so maybe have secrets?! – but somehow I suspect not.

Some people seem to have little regard for any rights or wrongs of having an affair, and regularly are unfaithful. Others – it seems to happen because they find a strong mutual attraction; they did not actually seek the relationship until the attraction becomes strong.

Affairs can be sometimes enriching in that partners can find a fulfilment and enjoyment not still found in their marriage, but I suspect that the hurt and the anger rather outweigh this in most cases. If partners never discover the affair, there is of course a better chance of a positive outcome; but I am sure far more partners at least suspect (if not know for sure) about the affair than ever say so. It may be better, not to acknowledge it – chances are that the errant husband or wife will return, then life can largely return to the previous position (though never the same of course).

Affair No. 1: It happened in 1971. I was 28 and in some ways rather naïve. I had just moved to a new town (not where I live now). I was on my own, and a neighbouring couple were very kind and befriended me. I had moved into a newly built bungalow and they helped a lot as I tackled it and a rather overgrown garden. I had known them for two to three months when I started the affair with the husband. With hindsight I can see that a feeling between us had been building up in a rather simple and innocent way. I had not at that time had any serious sexual relationship so I was rather naïve about what I was getting into. He, I suspect, was flattered and probably never intended anything more than enjoyable and flattering flirting.

We had worked together on the national census and when the work was completed he suggested we go for a drink together one evening to celebrate. It was during the conversation I became aware of a sexual attraction; he stopped the car on the way home, and kissed me.

I was visiting the house regularly, and baby-sitting sometimes for them. He would visit my home every week or so, he told his wife he was walking to the pub for a drink. After a few weeks we started having sex. We kidded ourselves that no-one else knew, but I suspect the neighbours did!

It fizzled out after about three or four months. We could never go out together, he could stay for only a very short time when he came to see me. This soon became very depressing and frustrating for me. I believe he soon felt very guilty about deceiving his wife – he was a decent man who had not set out to have an affair, he just got carried away. I told him it would be better if he did not come round any more, and he seemed a little relieved when I said it. I saw far less of the family after that, and I continued to live at the house for another four years.

The aftermath for me was serious depression on and off for most of those years. I was very unhappy. I was alone, and emotionally in a turmoil. I was immature and my first experience of sex, after the mutual euphoria, was frustrating and disappointing. They stayed together – I have not seen or heard of them since I moved away over twenty years ago.

Affair No. 2: This was rather different and lasted for several years. When it started I was 41, he was 48. He had been married since he was 21, and, I believe, had had no other affairs. As with my first affair, he was not a philanderer, and the affair was very slow to get off the ground. It was not his style and I still had bad memories of last time. I knew him through my job which took me to local authorities. He held a senior post, head of his department, and I had regular need to discuss matters with him. I had known him this way for six to seven years, for which time we had just seemed to 'hit it off'; I enjoyed talking to him – our conversations always lasted far longer than was needed for work and covered many matters. Looking back I can see that he was keeping me talking to keep me there! And I was happy to go along with this.

I remember one (long) conversation after which I became aware that I was attracted to him. I had no expectation of it leading anywhere, and I simply enjoyed the feeling. I began to take advantage of any opportunity to see him (always at work), and after a few more months I began to sense the feelings were mutual. Then one Saturday afternoon he rang me up at home, for a chat. I was a bit frosty with him – suddenly I was having to face up to what was happening and I was a little frightened. He said, next time he saw me, that he was sorry to have bothered me, but I said it was all right. Over the next months he rang me several times. Eventually, after this slow start, we went out for a drink one night. He had dropped hints which I picked up – it was largely my suggestion. It was, of course, all secret – but he lived several miles from me and none of my neighbours knew who he was. He told his wife he was visiting a colleague for the evening. We went to a country pub a few miles away and when he got back to the car he kissed me and that was the beginning of the affair proper. He came back to the house, we did not have full sex, but the 'scene was set'.

I saw him at work the following week, when he said he had some plants for the garden he had promised me. I suggested he bring them to the house, and he agreed to come the following evening. We both knew what it meant. When he came we had sex for the first time together. It was very happy, relaxed and loving, and after this he visited me regularly for some five years or so. We could never go out together of course. For the last eighteen months to two years the visits became less frequent. Somehow it just fizzled out. There was no argument. I had got rather bored and I suspect he had too. In such constricted circumstances it is impossible to keep a relationship alive and interesting. I am surprised it went on as long as it did.

We loved each other – he was the only really serious love in my life. I feel now (six years after it finished) rather like a bereaved wife. There was some pain after it ended. In different circumstances (i.e. if he had not been married)

I would have loved to marry him, we would have got along well, but it was not to be. I would not have missed the affair for anything, I have many happy warm memories. I have not seen him since his last visit. I still sometimes find myself wondering how he is, what he is doing.

There was never any consideration of his leaving his wife – it was never mentioned and I would never have expected it. I could never have lived with that. They are still together. They now have a new grandchild, I have heard. I am satisfied that it stayed secret – there are those at work who would have spread the story had they known, but this never happened. Of course, I will never know if his wife suspected anything.

For me it was a very positive experience – without it I would have had no meaningful or lasting sexual experience. It was a maturing experience, I suppose it was a substitute marriage for me.

It has been a strange experience writing about this – it is literally the first time I have told anyone about the affairs. I shared them with no-one else. When I finish writing this I shall post it to you immediately this evening – I do not like the idea of anyone else reading it. It is still private.

I have just re-read my first comments on page 1 [of her response to the MO directive, 'Having an Affair'] – and they seem strange now that I have pointed out my experiences on paper. Writing now I would not be so hard! Perhaps I am still more mixed up than I realized.

Autumn 2000, aged 57: The word 'family' to me has only the basic meaning of relating to my immediate biological family. I am the only one who, to some extent, escaped from the family. My siblings moved out when they married, but I left when I was 22, in 1966. I left the family home (near Northampton) and found a small flat on my own in town. I was only 5 miles away but it felt like a world away. Life with my parents – the others had all left by then – was stifling and depressing. I led a fairly quiet life in the flat but at least I was far more relaxed and I began to mature and develop in a way I had not until then. My job moved me away to East Anglia in 1970 which was when I first bought my own house. In one sense, I could say that was when I first became independent.

As far as I am aware the only example of someone being gay or lesbian in the family was an uncle, my father's brother. He died in 1971 aged 61. He never married, and lived on his own in Nottingham. He was very discreet and I would have thought his inclinations were not obvious to others. Looking back, it is surprising the way the matter was quietly accepted in the family – it was not an issue, it was not a cause of embarrassment. My parents, like many of their generation, were strict and 'old-fashioned' in their ideas especially on matters of sex, but I recall that on the odd occasions that his situation was mentioned they were very relaxed about it. They just seemed to accept it. As I grew up I suppose I absorbed the same attitudes. It was only later as an adult that others regarded it differently.

My uncle was artistically talented – he was a very good pianist, good enough to have been a professional had he wanted. He was also very good at needlework. I have still some pieces which he sewed. It is interesting that as I write this I am conscious that I am commenting on characteristics in a way which could be seen as stereotyping, indeed I was tempted to leave them unrecorded in case it was seen that way. But surely that would have been worse.

He had a clerical job in an office until his sudden death. He lived at home with my grandparents until they died, and then got the flat. He had a particular friend in later years – I know very little about him, but the family has always presumed that he too was gay. They never lived together but in adjoining flats. His death was from a heart attack, no doubt brought on from being a heavy smoker all his adult life.

Autumn 2006, aged 63: One of the lovely discoveries of getting to late middle age is to realize that I am not yet old. I suppose that when I was much younger I had expected to be in my dotage after I retired. In fact leaving what had become a boring and stressful job gave me a new lease of life. I feel younger now, nine years after retiring, than I did in my last years at work. But then there is so much more available now. Relative affluence means I have a car to get around in, I can afford books, I can live in comfort. I can study if I wish. All these help to keep your mind alert, and this is 90% keeping young. But – individuals have to make the effort to do new things, no one will ever do it for you.

A few years ago I picked up a flyer in the public library advertising a meeting to set up a group. The idea was to get going a 'think tank' to raise issues concerning older people in the area, with the intention of passing this on to government depts. This seemed very interesting and I went along to the inaugural meeting. There were some 100 or so older people there, and reps from the County Council. I went to a few later meetings but I realized I had been mistaken in its purpose – the only officials who were going to hear comments were County Council social workers (doing a bit of market research) and the issues were low-key local items and, tellingly, of most interest to older pensioners.

When setting up the group they asked for people over 50 to get involved – i.e. those approaching retirement. In reality all the issues discussed were of concern to older pensioners, and were very local, they were not wider issues as I had hoped. Ok, I got it wrong, but it illustrates an issue still not really noticed even by social services. The whole age-range of pensioners includes people of very different backgrounds and needs. It is silly to lump together all those aged between 50 and 90 or 100! That age range covers at least two generations, and those generations are very diverse.

Although I am a couple of years older than them I identify strongly with the post-war baby-boom generation who are right now coming up to retirement.

Apart from the fact of being retired we have little in common with older pensioners when it comes to attitudes, aspirations and expectations, income levels, life experiences. As most of us are still reasonably fit and active, services for the less active are not a major issue yet. However these are the sort of matters that social services automatically associate with anyone who has retired, whatever their age. The matters taking up most of the time at the local pensioners group were the availability of public lavatories and bus services. Of course these are important matters but not of grave import to a sixty-year old!

People of my age have lived very different lives to those now aged 80, especially the women most of whom have been to work (usually from choice) and had an independence and equality not available to their mothers. Most of us learned to drive a car and appreciate the freedom it gives us. Most women of our mothers' generation relied on husbands to chauffeur them about and expect that to go on. We have learned to speak up for ourselves, whereas many older women expect husbands to deal with matters. As we get older and start to do battle with e.g. social services we will be a generation far less docile and accepting, not so thankful for the crumbs thrown to us but making our own demands.

Without doubt no pensioner should be expected to live on the basic state pension, and even with tax credits income levels are too low. But surely the only way to persuade any government of any party to make sizeable increases is to accept that many pensioners these days do not need a state pension to survive. ...

I get angry at the way the question of means testing is treated by some people. It is not only stupid and misleading, but also cruel, to perpetuate the tales about how means testing was carried out in the bad old days, implying that it is still done that way. The methods of the nineteen-thirties were horrible and unforgivable. But that was three generations ago! Why keep jumping up and down on these nerve-ends? In no conceivable way are questions dealt with in that way today, but to hear some people talk you would think they were. Sadly it is often those who claim to be helping older people who are the worst at keeping the fears going. ...

In any case there is a simple and less worrying way to use means testing. Use the system which was, I believe, used for family allowances some years ago. Make the pension available to all (so there is no visible distinction between pensioners) but when total income is above a predetermined level the amount of the pension gets clawed back in tax. Or is this too simple? It puts the Age Concern moaners out of a job, but that is all to the good. I am afraid that I sometimes get cynical enough to believe the old adage about how carers have their own agendas to keep people dependent. ...

I cannot understand the argument that says that those who are fortunate enough to earn a bit more are entitled to keep it all just because they were fortunate. My views are almost communist in this – to those in need, and from those who can afford it …

Politicians are beginning to realize that they need to chat up the older generation because we are the only age-group who can be relied upon to turn out to vote. Unfortunately this will probably mean pandering to the lobby against tax increases …

Do we respect older people? In some ways we are getting better e.g. it is easier now for older people to be employed if they wish. I believe that the generation coming into the pensioner group now (the post-war generation) will be more prepared to speak up and demand what they want. Those now in the older age-ranges have often been too submissive and quiet …

How we are treated in the future will also depend on a sort of two-way movement. We have a right to demand high standards of care but we must also accept that this has to be paid for with higher taxation.

Winter 2008, aged 65: I find myself quietly getting more and more worried about the financial situation, especially about how we may be affected in future years. My finances are OK at the moment, but my former overall feelings of security have rather dissipated. This did not happen immediately the banks started collapsing but has crept up on me gradually.

I am retired so I am not worried about losing my job, though the numbers already out of work (with I am sure many more to come) are frightening. I have not heard yet of anyone I know losing their job, but then many of my contacts are fellow pensioners. (Since writing the above my next-door neighbour, who runs a small business, has said that they have had to lay off all but four of their twelve staff because of a lack of orders.)

While I realize that my pension is more secure than many it is still a concern for the longer-term. It is a public sector pension – I worked for the Audit Commission, and they set up their own pension fund when they were established in 1984. It is not however backed by public funds; it stands alone and must survive in a shaky stock market. If there were to be a major meltdown of the markets the fund would collapse. When I joined the Commission in 1984 it was by transfer from the Civil Service (the District Audit service) and I had the option of keeping my existing pension in the CS or transferring to the new fund. I moved to the new fund as a gesture of confidence in it. If I had kept my pension in the CS I would feel more confident now.

However it is a bit of a myth amongst people employed in the private sector that all so-called 'government' pensions are absolutely safe and secure. They are certainly more secure than many private-sector funds, but if times get really bad I am certain that public sector pensioners will suffer also. As has always happened with public sector pay, we will be required to set the example for others and e.g. accept that increases would stop or be curtailed. Of course this is not anywhere near as bad as losing one's pension pot just before retirement, but we do not have, and have never had, the level of security that outsiders imagine.

One possibility that is worrying is that state pensions could be means-tested. It is an idea that in some ways I cannot deny – they are now paid to many people who have comfortable incomes. But, again if things get really bad, at what level will the limits be? Many people could find their circumstances noticeably reduced by such a move. They would not be in poverty but would have to live quieter lives.

My regular shopping routine has not changed yet. Maybe this is because my income has not changed. I spent the usual amount this recent Christmas, and I am not planning changes to my purchasing habits. However, I find myself worrying whether my savings are secure and therefore whether I can afford major expenses which would be made from the savings. To date I have not needed to make such payments but I suspect I would think longer and harder if it should be necessary. I am needing to do some refurbishments in the kitchen soon and I find that almost unconsciously I am thinking of a smaller scheme than was done last time – not a complete new kitchen but only some new equipment and tiles to brighten it up. The idea of using part of my savings is a bit more of a concern than it would have been a year or two ago.

I paid off my mortgage several years ago so at least that is not a worry – I should be safe in my own home. Savings are another matter. It is probably true that the major loss in the current situation is confidence; we who had believed that we had been careful and saved for old age and invested conservatively to keep it secure are now not so secure. Most of my savings are in cash, with only about £25,000 in unit trusts. These latter are losing value but the cash, currently in a high interest account, is reasonably secure, or at least as secure as anything at the moment. It is in an account supposedly backed by the government; just how strong that guarantee can be remains to be seen!

I suppose the real answer [to how well the Government has handled the world financial crisis of 2008] is to wait and see how well we and the rest of the world survive it all. The real work has gone on behind the scenes, especially in the early days. Someone (and it can only be Goron Brown) did amazing things to get all the major countries cooperating to e.g. reduce interest rates on the same day – how he got China to agree to take part I will never know. His 'networking' with world leaders over the years really paid off.

Winter 2009, aged 66: Mid-life transitions – what is this? Maybe it is only a sudden awareness of what has been going on throughout our lives, but we notice it more at a time when we are conscious of getting a bit older, of time passing. All life is a transition, we get a bit older every day – but we hardly think about it when we are younger. Later comes a moment when we realize that changes will happen whether we like it or not, and we do not like to feel out of control. Such things congregate in middle age – retirement, getting to be officially old and getting a bus pass, hair turning grey – and this leads to an awareness that great parts of our lives are over. We have to admit we are mortal.

Mention is always made, for women, of the menopause. But I think this is only another of the inevitable changes in middle age mentioned above. Far too much is made of the fact that a woman can no longer have children – let's face it, how many sixty-year-old women want to start all that again? Much better to be a grandmother and choose just when you want to see the infant, and you can send them home when they get obstreperous!

I cannot remember how I found out about the menopause. I had been aware of it since I was young. When I realized it was happening to me, aged 52 to 54, I was aware of some expected changes, but thankfully I did not have serious physical symptoms. I had a few hot flushes for about nine months or so, and my periods just lessened and stopped. I had wondered about taking HRT but after reading up about it in an article in the *Guardian* I decided I would only take it if I had any very unpleasant symptoms. This did not happen. I did not fancy swallowing lots of artificial hormones for years just to pretend I was younger than I really was.

These days, thank heavens, it is easier and more acceptable to mention such subjects. When I was young, women seemed to pretend they did not happen; no wonder many women suffered problems in silence – they had little option. It makes it much easier for it to be talked about and explained within families and this must be helping to get new generations of menfolk more aware of what goes on around them. More openness makes it possible for women to seek reliable medical help, instead of having to rely on highly dubious, maybe even dangerous, gossipy information.

Winter 2009, aged 66: I have heard uninspiring things about book groups – only a few members actually bother to get and read the books and talk about them, many people come along but never join in, and this is not the sort of group I would want to join. Many of them, too, only seem to read modern light fiction. Still, I learned a huge amount from Jean, our tutor [on a WEA literature class covering European and modernist literature], and this will always be with me.

Age Group – how represented – as I read hardly any modern fiction it is difficult to see how I can answer this. I am presuming you are thinking of current fiction.

Films and TV – I have in recent years noticed a change in the representation of women generally. They are now very likely to be shown as strong and assertive, to the exclusion of any representations of other types of women! Perhaps we have only changed one stereotype for another. Instead of showing quiet and compliant women, as was the norm when I was younger, it is now almost compulsory to show the opposite. This is very noticeable in TV adverts.

When it comes to pensioners there is the widespread stereotype (over eighty and penniless) and far less recognition of younger pensioners, many of whom are quite comfortably off. This reflects the general attitudes of society. There is however one type of TV drama series which seems to be aimed at the sixty-somethings – where the younger generation can only manage if the oldies move back in and do things as they used to when they were working. Series such as *New Tricks* (retired policemen come back to solve old cases to show up the youngsters who failed to do so) and *A Touch of Frost* where the unbelievably old, always-successful detective is of the old school and unable to work a computer. He is a totally unrealistic character but I suppose he is there just to let the sixty-somethings feel smug about their former working methods. I find the idea behind these really rather sad; they seem to be for people who cannot move with the times and forget that they were given early retirement because their ideas and methods were not good enough. I suppose they are reassured by the plots in the series. But is this really how pensioners want to be portrayed – as people unable to move with the times, and content to be seen as this? It bothers me if they do.

It can be depressing when groups that should know better, e.g. Age Concern, persist with the 'old and penniless and a bit dim' stereotype of older people. Pensioners can be aged fifty-something or one hundred and something, a difference of over two generations, and yet we are nearly always lumped together as one group. The younger ones have had different life experiences, they frequently have higher income levels, different and more assertive attitudes, and yet we are still presented as all alike. If a new Government form is brought out you can guarantee someone from Age Concern will start wittering about how 'pensioners' will not be able to fill it in. Excuse me, but I am quite capable of filling in a form despite my advanced age. Please do not presume that I am incapable simply because I am older.

There was a very interesting discussion programme on Radio 4 the other night, about promoting the idea of abolishing what they called middle-class benefits – not paying benefits to those who do not need them. The remit of this programme was to discuss how this could be promoted in this country (as it has been in others) and whether voters would accept it. It was deliberately provocative to get the comments coming from the MPs and economists on the programme. It is reckoned that we could save some £7 billion a year by not paying e.g. winter fuel allowance, free bus passes and child allowance to people on hard times. Apparently our welfare state spends more than any other in the western world on benefits for those who do not need them! I have heard much discussion amongst pensioners about how stupid it is to pay the winter fuel allowance to so many people who do not by any description need it. The general feeling on the programme was that it would be almost impossible to get past the voters – and sadly I think they were right. Although there would be a bank of people seeing the sense and fairness of it I think most people are just too greedy to give up their freebies.

The above programme was a hopeful sign that perhaps MPs might be beginning to see pensioners as not one homogeneous group, but as varied individuals. I suspect there is still a long way to go.

10

'The Young Do Not Have Exclusive Rights to Love and Happiness'

Joanna Woods

*J*oanna Woods *was born in 1943, the only child of a working-class family. She had neither the money nor support to pursue higher education and left her local grammar school at sixteen. She later completed a degree in her fifties by evening study. Joanna enjoyed her work as a university administrator and was reluctant to retire. She was worried that retirement signalled the end of her 'usefulness' and that she would feel like a 'non-person' without the stimulation and social contact. Her experience has proven otherwise. Joanna belongs to the WEA, socializes with friends and makes the most of concession passes to the theatre and swimming pool. She enjoys having more time to spend with her husband now that they're not working. Joanna reflects on the immense rewards of being a grandparent but feels that radically changing parenting methods create a lot of potential for conflict. She considers the problem of 'involuntary' grandparenting:*

> 'Most grandparents enjoy "helping out", but there are a growing number who have no choice. How fair is this? If money is not desperate, are these "liberated women" pursuing their careers at the expense of their parents' own peaceful retirement? Young people seem to expect them to be unpaid childminders which I think is rather unfair at a time when they should be enjoying their freedom or are often looking after their own husband or wife.'

Joanna was a carer for her elderly aunts and her mother, and therefore has 'a lot of empathy with the elderly and also the conflicting emotions of a carer'. She admits that having her elderly mother live with her was a strain on her marriage. While she has two sons, one of them lives abroad, and she has no other relatives. This makes her anxious about dying alone: 'The days of the extended family are largely gone among the English.' Joanna thinks that older people should have access to computing lessons to prevent their social marginalization. The title of this chapter is taken from her reflections on the tragedy of losing a life partner, and the importance of love and companionship in old age: 'The young do not have exclusive rights to love and happiness.'

As discussed in the introduction and the appendix to this book, Joanna's account is taken from the autobiographical life history she wrote for FCMAP and some of the responses from her reading dairy.

On retirement: I have friends who I can socialize with including one or two ex-work colleagues so I do not feel isolated at all. I take advantage of concessions at the theatre etc. and recently the free swimming for the over 60s. I love my freedom pass which I use regularly although I must admit that I get a little miffed when the bus conductor doesn't even bother to ask me for it! Also, I have mixed feelings when a young person offers me their seat – although of course I accept gracefully.

I was a little reluctant to join the U3A, as I felt it was admitting I was 'old,' and usually resist joining things specifically for one type of person. However, I already belong to the WEA which although a mixed aged group, has members in their 70s and 80s with razor sharp minds and I have always found older people very interesting with so much experience of life to share.

Most grandparents enjoy 'helping out,' but there are a growing number who have no choice. How fair is this? If money is not desperate, are these 'liberated women' pursuing their careers at the expense of their parents' own peaceful retirement? Young people seem to expect them to be unpaid childminders which I think is rather unfair at a time when they should be enjoying their freedom or are often looking after their own husband or wife.

On being a carer for her two elderly, unmarried aunts and her mother: I have a lot of empathy with the elderly and also the conflicting emotions of a carer. The older sister had a stroke and was in a nursing home for two years, unable to speak. This was the first time that the realities of growing old really hit me. It was such a depressing place, and many of the residents had no visitors at all.

The days of the extended family are largely gone among the English. I am lucky to have my health and a reasonable income to do the things I enjoy, although not enough to be free of worry about what will happen if either my husband or I have to go into care. There is a great resentment that the elderly are made to sell their houses to fund their care and this situation needs to be addressed.

On the importance of love and companionship in old age: The young do not have exclusive rights to love and happiness.

Reading diaries: Joanna's reflections on ageing

Joanna's reading diaries reflect very many of her own experiences of ageing, older people whom she had known and of conditions such as loneliness, deafness and dementia that affect them. David Lodge's Deaf Sentence *in particular produced a veritable outpouring of personal recollection in Joanna, and a range of other reflections on life, as can be seen below. Additionally after the reading group discussion, she reflected for instance that it demonstrated much about older men, both on the part of Desmond the increasingly deaf protagonist, a recently retired academic, and his even older father, as opposed to the implied vitality of older women. The edited material is synthesized in the narrative below.*

It was felt that Desmond's view of ageing was a pessimistic one, – he was depressed, critical, withdrawn from life and bitter. He felt rejected by his wife and was an example of one of the dangers of retirement – that you give up. It was thought that this was more prevalent among males and might explain why so few joined the U3A compared to women. Men were reluctant to discuss their personal feelings and tend to define themselves by their work.

Although it may be difficult for some of us to understand Dad's [i.e. Desmond's father's] reluctance to spend any money to make his life more bearable, it was argued by one group member that the older person's attitude to money is a bulwark against their need for independence. Their over-riding fear is to lose control of any aspect of their lives, and this is one way of retaining it. The eldest member of the group was sorry that she could no longer drive – another example of a loss of independence.

One lady talked about the 'throwaway' generation. Those of us who had grown up either during or just after the war were far more conscious of thrift and the avoidance of waste.

A grandmother remarked that we are much younger nowadays in our attitudes and looks, and that often leads to our children expecting too much of us – they don't realize that although we feel young in our head, our bodies are slowing down and get tired quicker than they used to.

Unfortunately our only grandchild lives abroad, but most of my friends spend a great deal of time with theirs. However, that grandparents are much older than they were in the past, due to women having children much later, and although they enjoy being with their grandchildren, they find it very tiring. Young people seem to expect them to be unpaid child-minders which I think is rather unfair at a time when they should be enjoying their freedom or are often looking after their own husband or wife. However, I would dearly love to have my grandson with me, and would perhaps change my views!

It is true that grandparents can 'spoil' their grandchildren. There is usually a great affinity between the older and youngest generation. They do not feel the responsibility as they did when parents. However, I have to say that on the question of discipline, many of my friends feel as I do, that parenting methods have changed so radically that we have to be very careful not to criticize our children for being too lenient on their own children and for lavishing too much attention on them. I wonder if this applies to every generation.

I went on an excellent retirement course arranged by the university which helped to allay my fears, and in the event, after six months I suddenly felt that the time had come and saw retirement as a chance to do so many things other than work. Since the day I retired I have never regretted it. I was grateful that my employers had removed the compulsion to retire at 65 – I felt that the fact that I made my own decision helped me to adjust to retirement much more easily. On the other hand, I can understand the concerns that unemployment among the young would be increased if all workers could stay on indefinitely. But older people have a lot to offer and many people in the future will not be able to afford to retire, especially if the state pension age is raised.

My father died suddenly at 54, and although this was untimely and a very great shock, my memory of him was that he was already 'an oldish man'. He was intelligent but uneducated and he had settled for a secure but low paid job when he was orphaned at 13. There was no job satisfaction and he only saw it as a means of supporting his family. He looked forward to his retirement, but in a negative way – i.e. not having to go to work, rather than seeing it as an opportunity to pursue other interests.

Unfortunately given my father's early death, he and my mother relied very much on each other for their social life resulting in my mother having to make a supreme effort to make friends when he was gone. This she did by returning to work and joining an 'over fifties club'. As she grew older though, she became more and more dependent on me for company. I think it is probably easier for women when they are left alone, although the next generation of men will be more able to look after themselves in terms of cooking etc.

Mother had moved to a flat suitable for the elderly when she was in her eighties. One day she panicked when crossing the road and from that day never ventured out on her own. When I asked social services for help with my mother, they came round when I was not there, and she told them that she didn't need any help as 'her daughter did everything'. She lived about an hour from me, so it was most sensible for her to move in with us.

When my mother came to live with us, she was determined 'not to be a burden.' She was sweet natured and whilst she was able, tried to help in the house. My husband was brilliant, but it did cause problems between us for example when she would empty the dishwasher before it was washed and clatter about when he was trying to make phone calls. Although she lived with us for twelve years, I would never condemn anyone who could not have their parents to live with them. I also looked after a maiden aunt whom I loved to death, but could never have lived with. I got on very well with my mother, and it was only during the last few years that we began to resent our lack of a 'life' and privacy. I had such overwhelming conflicting loyalties to my husband and her, and would hate my children to be put in the same position.

I have to say though, that when my mother had to have almost constant care and an army of helpers, she was usually very appreciative. I found the carers mostly very sensitive, although it was difficult to find one who struck the right balance between sitting passively by her side and over-enthusiastically trying to stimulate her with games, songs etc. when she was obviously not feeling up to it. Although the council provided limited care, we had to pay for most of it – the alternatives would have been for me to give up my job, or find a care home. Living so much longer, carers themselves are too old to perform these duties unaided and often on very little income. The ideal would be if everyone could afford a 'granny flat' or to live very close to their parents.

My mother was quite deaf and it was very frustrating for both of us. She often pretended to hear me and then denied that I had said something. It is true that people are quite understandably more sympathetic to the blind. My mother struggled with her National Health aid – as her fingers became less nimble it was impossible for her to maneuver it without help, and the more sophisticated ones, had she been able to afford them, would have been just as difficult. One in six people need help with hearing but only 17% of the deaf wear hearing aids. I think many people feel there is a stigma attached to wearing one – possibly accompanied by a feeling that one is growing old. Research into more effective, affordable and discreet hearing aids is vital. I was sent some information on a guide 'Hearing Aids – your rights explained,' but it was from a commercial company, no doubt with ulterior motives. Desmond comments that the words deaf and death are often misheard by the hearing impaired and that 'Deafness is a kind of pre-death. ... A long staircase leading down to the grave'. Thus, I wonder, do all deaf people feel that they are ageing prematurely?

My mum used to say 'you are my mum now'. It is an extraordinary experience which takes the infant/parent relationship through the taboo barrier. My mother had two carers at one point – one was perfectly kind, but sat passively all day making no attempt to converse or stimulate her. The other was over 'jolly' and wanted her to engage in activities all day long which was too much for a ninety-six-year old! They both meant very well, but did not have the sensitivity to see the needs of the patient. Such people are probably very rare and precious.

Increasing expectation of life due to medical advances does not seem to be matched by an increasing ability to enjoy ones later years. I think Desmond's own deafness and feeling of being 'redundant' from any useful purpose, paints a rather pessimistic picture of ageing. His wife is not so much younger but has in fact a fulfilled and busy life, as have many older people nowadays. However, any disability or health problem plays an enormous factor in one's ability to enjoy later life. But so does attitude.

I worked in a university until earlier this year. Although on the administrative staff, I had a close connection with students and lecturers, as my job involved running workshops and preparing students for their sandwich work placements, and had frequent contact with industry. My university recently removed the compulsion to retire at 65, and as that time approached, I began to feel very nervous about the thought. I enjoyed my job, and know exactly what Desmond means about the rhythms of the academic year. I had a good deal of job satisfaction and was very attached to the students although it became an increasing challenge to find them jobs in the current climate. I had heart surgery in early 2008 and was due to retire in August. There was a great deal of pressure from my family and friends to retire, but I supposed I felt that this would be admitting that I was 'old'. I think many of us define ourselves by our work to a certain extent, and that must be even truer with an academic of considerable renown. I definitely would have resented it if I had been forced to retire at 65, even though I made the decision a few months later and have not regretted it.

My husband retired in 2006 at the age of 67 having been self-employed all his life with similar misgivings. We have never been able to spend enough time together, so that was one of the main factors in my decision, when I finally made it. Also we have a son and grandson living in America and wanted to spend more than the usual two weeks with them.

The question of compulsory retirement at 65 is a controversial one. Older people have so much to offer, so why should they be put on the scrap heap at 65? And in the future, who will be able to afford to retire then even if they so wish? It is true that one must consider youth unemployment and address that issue as an argument against raising the retirement age. An ideal scenario is that policies be formed so that people can be given the CHOICE according to their circumstances.

Recent *Woman's Hour* programmes have reported that employers are actually giving incentives such as health care to encourage older women to stay on in the workforce – MacDonald's found that employing women over 69 boosted customer satisfaction. Older employees both male and female often have a stronger work ethic, better customer skills and maturity. Small businesses like the flexibility of not having to employ women of child bearing years with the associated maternity benefits and the work is often part time and low paid. Some 'baby boomers' who expected to rely on their husbands for pensions, took breaks to have children, and did not pay the full 'stamp', are going to end up with a very reduced pension and will be forced to work for much longer than they wish.

I think the freedom pass is a huge benefit for the retired person. It enables us to make frequent visits to London to the theatre and museums etc. which would be beyond our means. There has been some talk in the press recently that some senior citizens are 'abusing' their bus passes by using them on long trips when they could perfectly afford to pay. I think if the government was to stop such concessions it would be a sad day for the elderly and severely restrict their quality of life.

Old people cling onto past possessions and seem so reluctant to spend any money making life more bearable. Is this because they have experienced hardship during their youth and can't break the habit? Even people with reasonable incomes seem to resist paying for things that were considered 'extravagant' in their youth. For example, my auntie refused to pay for a taxi to take her three miles to a free Christmas party. Dad averts his eyes when Des pays the taxi fare 'as if it was a transaction too shameful to witness.'

I had an experience with my aunt where, although I had said I didn't want her resuscitated, the doctor tried to tell me that she had refused a certain treatment which would have given her a chance of recovery. Before her fall, she had had a good quality of life and I resisted his implication that it would be better not to treat her. I knew that her slight dementia meant that she could not have made an informed choice on the subject. He agrees to ask her again in my presence – she agreed and recovered enough to live a reasonably happy life for several more years. I do appreciate that doctors have impossible decisions to make. The treatment involved taking up a bed in a high dependency unit which I suppose he felt should be left free for a younger person. What I really resented was that he put words in the mouth of an elderly lady who was incapable of fully understanding the situation. I really fear for people who have no one to speak on their behalf.

My auntie's neighbours had regarded her as an irritation in their totally uneventful lives. Another couple used to collect her and bring her back from old time dancing. This was kind, but it was not out of their way. One night she had not appeared at the bottom of the flats. Instead of going to see what was wrong, they had just driven on. She had actually collapsed on the floor and was not found until much later. Perhaps we are all guilty of un-neighbourliness and the English trait of 'keeping ourselves to ourselves'.

People do tend to group the 'elderly' together, not bothering to look at them as individuals. And to label 'the elderly' as one group is obviously a simplification. People seem to have no problems with respecting and honouring those who have achieved great things – a recent example is the war veterans. Old men such as Berlesconni often make fools of themselves. Money, class and education cause just as many gulfs amongst the elderly as between young and old. Retirement homes for the well-heeled differ greatly from those which are council run. However, they are not necessarily more inviting. My auntie was sent for a short period of rehabilitation into a home which closely resembled a five star hotel. However, there was no warmth in the atmosphere and to me it was very impersonal and regimented. When we moved her permanently to a much less palatial environment, she was surrounded by efficient but caring people and was as happy as one could be in such an establishment. It is easier for a naturally sociable person to adapt to residential care. I can appreciate how abhorrent it would be to some to be jollied along into playing bingo and such like.

As senior citizens, we are not powerless to change things. We can engage in lobbying and campaigning and join organizations such as Amnesty International. There are many examples of the elderly making a difference. One is that of a wonderful woman called Doctor Hamlyn who at the age of 85 is still saving girls in Ethiopia from fistula, where they are treated as outcasts by their families. I do think Lodge presents old age in a rather negative way.

The reading and discussion groups inspired a wide range of interesting ideas and reflections in Joanna's other reading diaries; these included some key rhetorical questions with which this section commences:

Do people play the 'age' card to avoid unpleasant tasks?

When does 'old age' begin?

What motives do people actually have for helping others? Mixed, if we are honest – does it make us feel needed? Whatever the reasons, the elderly need to be helped in a way that is not patronizing and leaves them with their dignity.

What are our motives for giving to charity? Are we more inclined to donate to causes we can relate to? Does this mean that Help the Aged and such like only attract people who are involved with the elderly in some way?

I wonder why more women seem to attend church than men. It is true that old women often are in the majority. This is particularly noticeable in Greek Orthodox churches. Do they just find it a comfort in their widowhood?

Many women, after the break-up of a long marriage, feel worthless and unattractive. Not a happy feeling to take into old age. A friend of mine's husband recently left her after forty years because 'he felt it was his last chance of happiness'. How much effort had he made to make his wife happy?

I feel with this project that I keep repeating myself, as the themes recur – but I personally am pleased to spend more time with my husband as it has been hard to do so while we were both working, particularly as he had his own business. However, we make sure that we pursue our own interests and try not to 'get under each other's feet'. I think if you have a basically sound relationship, you can adjust with some give and take on each side. If there are serious problems which have not been addressed – they come to a head as people are forced to spend more time together, become aware of their own mortality and frustrations and bitterness surface.

It's definitely harder to adapt to change as one grows older, which is why social workers are keen for the elderly to stay in their own homes for as long as they can. Old people are far more isolated now, especially in towns, unless they are able and inclined to visit day centres, some never speak to a soul from morning until night. I think the elderly who live in towns are far lonelier and more nervous of the young than those who live in the tight knit community of a village. Animals are a great comfort to the elderly, particularly cats as they are independent and it has been proved that it relieves stress to stroke them. My friend's cat used to spend the large part of the day on her elderly neighbours sofa, and she was devastated when he died.

Cooking a meal is such an important thing for the elderly or depressed to do. When my mother was widowed she was only in her fifties, but until well into her eighties she always cooked herself a proper meal, setting the table, and enjoying it. Apart from the health benefits she said it gave her something to do. Many old people keep a sense of control over their lives by completing household chores for as long as they can. As eyesight fails, their houses often become dirty – this happened to my mother, but she would have been appalled if she had known.

A friend in her 60s recently had a 'celebration of life' funeral, with bright colours and joyful singing. She had arranged it herself. It was very uplifting.

Of retirement people say: 'A woman can always find plenty to occupy herself'. In the 21st century this seems a sexist idea – usually implying household tasks etc. However, it can be true that men find retirement more difficult. They seem to form less close friendships and are not, on the whole 'joiners.' We see evidence of this in evening classes, even U3A meetings.

It must be the final insult to know that one's retirement was regarded as a blessing to the organization. I retired a year ago and had a good send off and happy memories. However, I have just discovered that my job has recently been virtually 'downgraded' by a review. If I had waited another year to retire, I think I would have felt very different and very undervalued, although I know in my heart the decision has affected many people and was not in any way personal slight.

Many elderly people had no opportunities for further education in their youth. Some may look back and wonder what difference this would have made to their lives. Fortunately there are many mature students who have taken advantage of the Open University etc.

It is wonderful that so many retired people now lead an active and fulfilling social life – but it can be insensitive to emphasize this in a self-congratulatory way to those who do not, making them feel even more useless and isolated. It is a bit like the 'stay at home housewife' being told they are boring and unfulfilled. Each person should be encouraged to find their own level of fulfillment.

Scrapbooks and photographs are so important to the elderly. I already enjoy looking through mine. I wonder what the advent of the digital camera will do. Most people don't even print their photographs now. I remember with a hallucinatory sensitivity, sense impressions, e.g. the taste of a bacon sandwich, the sensation of sunlight on my neck when first had haircut. I may have mentioned this before, but in the spring, my mother always kept a bowl of hyacinths in the hall when I was a child and the smell never fails to transport me back there.

In one meeting we discussed whether we should be valued for our memories. Many old people have rich experiences of such things as the holocaust which can illuminate younger people's perception of them. One member said that when she was relating her memories to her grandchildren, she always focused on the positive things. In another book group debate the most dominant theme [of Trezza Azzopardi's *Remember Me*] was thought to be how we edit our memories. They can be a great comfort to us especially when our friends start dying. We can remember the good times and forget the bad. A very good friend of mine died last week and I found this was very true. Also, we do not always know how much we actually remember and how much are things we have been told. I recently met some old school friends who remembered things about me that I had no recollection of whatsoever. At the book group we also talked about how important certain possessions become as we get older. They mark significant events in our lives. It is very sad when people have to go into care and cannot take their treasures with them. They can often be seen pouring over old photographs of loved ones. One member remarked about loss of memory and how people begin to judge you and become irritated if you struggle to find the right word. Even brilliant people tend to be patronized and treated like half-wits if they do not immediately grasp a point a younger person is making. We discussed how important it is not to make assumptions about people and put them into categories. However, we often catch ourselves referring to 'that old lady' or 'the elderly'. It is hard to admit that we are or soon will be, in that category. I am beginning to get tired of any ailment I have being attributed to 'age-related wear or deterioration'!

Both my mother and aunt had dementia in some degree, although not that severe. My mother sometimes used to tell small lies to avoid me 'telling her off' for a trivial misdemeanor. My mother used to love to read, and at first I thought it was her eyesight that made it increasingly hard to do so. The doctor told me that it has something to do with the difficulty that the brain has in interpreting the meaning of the words. My auntie who had spells of dementia but at times seemed perfectly lucid, frequently told the mini-cab bringing her home from a hospital appointment to drop her off at her previous address, and was found wandering the streets. This was despite my frequent complaints to the hospital and instructions not to deliver her to any other address than that given on her notes.

How important it is for anyone caring for someone, children, invalids or the elderly to have some respite. I think this is one of the most important priorities for the carers of an ageing population. I know when I cared for my mother, I felt refreshed even after a short time to myself and a weekend away was like a long holiday. There is a charity called Crossroads which funds such breaks but it is something the government should put high on the agenda.

I think with new technology many older people feel their existing skills, such as mental arithmetic, are just laughable. I often find myself relating how I had to add up many items in my head when working in a shop as a Saturday job. Electronic tills make this skill redundant as do calculators. In a recent exam at the university where I worked, a class of accountancy students was unable to do simple calculations without them. There is a definite need to provide classes to teach older people the simple computing skills which are necessary to avoid them becoming marginalized from society. I think it would be a good idea to let unemployed youngsters teach the elderly these skills – both groups would benefit.

Nostalgia for Joe Lyonses [in Angela Carter's *Wise Children*]. The description was pitch perfect. I read this out to my husband and he agreed. You only miss an institution like Joe Lyons when it's gone. Couldn't find a place to get a cup of tea. I've heard so many old people say this (do you remember Dad in Deaf Sentence). Starbucks and the like must seem so alien to the very old.

The elderly are often invisible to the young. A friend of mine has just told me that when she asked a young man recently to remove his feet from the seat in the underground where she wanted to sit, he replied that 'old people should all be killed off'. Worrying to say the least! Although these days, I think the elderly are mostly tolerated or ignored by the young. It depends on how well they have aged, and if they have managed to stay interesting and active. Maybe teenagers get embarrassed if their parents try to look and behave in manner considered 'too young'. But it is quite acceptable for the older generation not to 'act their age'. However, I personally do not think the obsession with face-lifts etc. is healthy. You can still 'grow old gracefully' and yet be young in heart. How cruel the young can be, albeit unintentionally. I don't think the media help with their constant images of beautiful youth. And now I am old, I think I know why grandma didn't like us at eighteen – we felt no irony. How easy we were impressed.

Certainly the young do not have exclusive rights to love and happiness. Indeed, many a people find love in later life especially with the advent of dating agencies. I know several such couples. It is so touching to see elderly married couples still so obviously in love. Sometimes you see an elderly couple sitting on a bench in companionable silence, and then walking away holding hands. There is no need for words. As people live longer, couples may have longer together – but then, how much harder it is when one of them dies. A young widow or widower can make a new life eventually, but for the elderly, to lose their life partner is often to lose the will to live. In my auntie's home was an old couple who had decided to go into care together – how much more bearable that must have been for them than for a person on their own.

One member raised the point that women for a long while in the post-war years found it very difficult to get a mortgage or borrow money. Even when I got married in 1965 they would only take half my salary into account as it was assumed I would have children soon and leave work. Mastectomy was not talked about it those days and many people were not even told that they had cancer. I think it is better to be open about these things so that people can talk about their fears and worries in an open atmosphere instead of constantly worrying what is wrong with them, sometimes without foundation.

At one reading group meeting a member said that they had become more afraid of the actual process of dying rather than dying itself. This is probably a result of seeing the suffering of their peers. We are all going to die. But we don't want to admit it. We don't realize how important everything and everyone is until it's taken away.

Afterword

ooking back on fifty years of the welfare state in 1995, Nicholas Timmins notes that among its legacies is the fact that 'life expectancy had climbed for men from around sixty at birth in the 1930s to seventy-three by 1991, with women at each stage expecting to live about five years longer' (499). He goes on, however, to point out that people were beginning to question 'whether the tide of elderly which had been rising steadily since the welfare state's foundation would finally overwhelm it' (519). While we can dispute that caricature of the 'silver tsunami' threatening to submerge health and social services by arguing that such characterizations fail to take account of both the economic production of those in the retired age ranges – many of whom continue to work or volunteer – and the amount of care they provide for other older people or younger generations such as grandchildren, perhaps a more productive way of looking at the various experiences of growing old in the welfare state described in this collection is to ponder in what way they complicate the wider debate identified by Timmins as beginning in the 1990s:

> A new debate was beginning, or perhaps an old one was being renewed, as to whether Britain was really an individualist's society, in which the collective provision of the post-Beveridge ere was something of an aberration, or whether Thatcherism, with its desire, but its failure, fundamentally to shift the boundaries, was the exception. (518)

What Timmins meant by writing that Thatcherism had failed to fundamentally shift the boundaries was that for all the rhetoric, recessions and reductions in public spending of the Thatcher years, there was still in place in the mid-1990s an effective – if sometime creaking – system of public health, social services and education to support the British population from cradle to grave. The question was whether that system could continue in the face of a paradigmatic change in the social and cultural values of the nation from the collective conformism of the early 1950s to the multiple individualist lifestyles of the 1990s?

In discussing the mass observer he calls Len in his *Seven Lives from Mass Observation* (2016) – whom here we call Dick Turpin – James Hinton describes his accounts as representative 'of the experience of large numbers of people caught between the hammer of the 1980s and the anvil of the 1960s' (93). That is to say he was equally alienated and upset by the sexual and feminist revolutions of the 1960s and the Thatcherite era of privatization, financial deregulation and destruction of the unions and manufacturing industry. Dick, as an example of a wider body of skilled manual labour (in his case a mechanic who moved into public sector transport supervision and management), manifests a nostalgia for pre-1955 Britain. Whereas the older way of life he values was once supported by the welfare state, it is the welfare state which in practice has undermined those values by enabling the social changes of both the 1960s and the 1980s to take place (this latter suggestion may seem counter-intuitive, but it would have been impossible for the Thatcher government to triple unemployment in the early 1980s without a safety net in place to largely catch the resultant social consequences). To satisfy Dick, it would logically require the combination of a collectivist welfare state with the repeal of some or most of the socially liberalizing legislation of the 1960s and the 1970s. This would suggest that the terms of the debate identified by Timmins in the 1990s have now shifted so that the collectivist and individualist positions which were respectively those of the political left and right in the 1990s might almost be considered to have changed places. From this perspective, in the post-Brexit-vote society we now inhabit, it is the left which is now aligned with individualism, often in the form of an identity politics, and the right seeking the return to a more traditional collectivism (albeit without strong trade unions) as evidenced by Theresa May in her first speech as Conservative leader and prime minister on 13 July 2016, when she sought to speak directly to the British working class:

> If you're from an ordinary working class family, life is much harder than many people in Westminster realise. You have a job but you don't always have job security. You have your own home but you worry about paying the mortgage. You can just about manage, but you worry about the cost of living and getting your kids into a good school. If you're one of those families, if you're just managing, I want to address you directly. I know you're working around the clock, I know you're doing your best and I know that sometimes life can be a struggle. The Government I lead will be driven, not by the interests of the privileged few, but by yours. We will do everything we can to give you more control over your lives. (May 2016)

On the other hand, in discussing the mass observer he calls Stella – whom here we call Beryl Saunders – Hinton points out an apparent paradox of 'a thoroughly engaged citizen for whom politics was largely a matter of indifference' (76). While Beryl's embrace of the emotional and sexual revolution, anti-psychiatry and 'New Age' alternative therapies suggests a rejection of traditional, collective values, Hinton suggests that the consequences were 'neither individualistic or normalizing':

> The alternative therapies with which she experimented were geared not to adjusting the individual to predetermined social roles, but to freeing them from the tyranny of norms so that 'any problem can be looked at honestly out in the open'. Freedom from norms was not, however, a recipe for anti-social individualism. [...] The ethos was co-operative, not individualistic, and Stella [Beryl] saw herself as participating in a human growth movement, in its own way a politics of social transformation. (76–77)

The deeper message here is that, in the logic that consciously informs Hinton's approach, by studying individual lives in detail, we gain an insight into the complex, interwoven historical strands that make up our present. Arguably, it is the apparent contradictions within lives that reveal the deficiencies of the cultural frameworks which we assume to be operating. Dick Turpin's deep unhappiness with the liberalizing changes of the 1960s did not draw him to the politics of Thatcher, even though she campaigned for a return to traditional values, because he identified her project of privatization as equally part of the assault on collective social values in the name of individualism. Beryl Saunders's marked preference for alternative psychology, group therapy and sexual and emotional liberation over politics might suggest an extreme form of individualism but actually seems to have been more in line with a form of collective social transformation. What links the stories of these two mass observers of almost identical age and other members of the interwar generation is that their stories suggest we need to rethink, or at least elaborate, the paradigms and interpretive frameworks by which we try and understand contemporary history. From this perspective, the defining characteristic of this generation is not so much a rejection of contemporary mores in Britain in favour of the attitudinal values of their youth, as a sense that contemporary Britain has either failed or not yet succeeded in changing the world of their youth into the transformed future that they sought to achieve throughout their lives by the activities they engaged in.

An objection to this line of argument might be raised along the lines that Dick does not want to change the world of his youth but return to it. However, the problem with this line of argument is that it undermines the complexity of these mass-observer lives by implying that they can be readily understood as binary-gendered responses. Hinton accounts for this apparent division well by arguing that while 'for most men of this [interwar] generation, gender was an unproblematic given', women were dependent on 'more complicated processes [to construct] their sense of themselves' (165). The difference is therefore not essentialist but a result of women being more likely to undertake a particular process of self-discovery than men because they wanted more from their lives than the subordinate roles they were offered in the 1940s and 1950s. There was nothing preventing men from following a similar path other than the fact that they already appeared to have clearly defined active social roles – as breadwinner, husband and father – openly available to them. In fact, we might see those men who did participate in MO as on some level seeking such a path of self-discovery as followed by many women. As Hinton argues, by describing himself as an 'old reactionary', Dick 'could be seen as a man who had internalised a narrow and life-denying subaltern consciousness' but, on the other hand, as 'an MO correspondent' he found a way nonetheless to explore much wider horizons (108).

Therefore, if we reject gender as the prime determinant of self-discovery in the name of a wider social transformation, how else might we broadly classify this lifelong process of self-reflexively considering our own experience in the world even as the social context constantly changes? The term that best covers this process in the context of this book is 'growing old'. Arguably, the acceptance by the mass observers that they are old is both an unavoidable product of their self-reflexive practice and acknowledgement that 'life has meaning because it ends but its end is not its meaning' and thus an acceptance and statement of their recognition that they are the authors of their own lives (Hubble and Tew 2013: 205). As Lynne Segal observes in *Out of Time: The Pleasures and Perils of Ageing* (2013): 'To the extent that we can manage it, awareness of mortality can enhance our sense of our bonds with others and our embrace of the moment' (170). Anne Karpf (2014) makes a similar point about the need to 'incorporate [our mortality] into our daily lives' (109) but also insists that 'we never need to lose our earlier selves only add to them' (55). This understanding is central to the lives recorded in this book, and arguably it is the reflective awareness of their past earlier selves that enables these MO diaries to expose the complex, multilayered composition of the contemporary present we inhabit. On such a reading, 'growing old' isn't just something that happens to us but something that we need to do both actively and self-reflectively. In *Ageing, Narrative and Identity*, we provide histories and analyses of MO and the U3A which suggest why these two organizations are particularly good in encouraging this process to take place, but the simplest explanation is – as demonstrated by the accounts included in this volume – that they embrace ageing as a lifelong process. As Karpf argues, this will not stop us eventually declining and dying but it will help us in the more difficult task of actually living:

In Western societies we tend to think of ageing as a biomedical terms, as a physiological condition. And of course we are embodied creatures, the state of our bodies as we age making certain activities possible and closing off others. But an equally, if not more, crucial factor shaping the way that we age is the culture in which we live: not only its attitude towards ageing, but also its policies. For swathes of people, getting older means getting poorer, which in turn leads to them being marginalised from the pleasures and plenitude of life. The more noisily we promote [an alternative] approach to ageing, one which embraces ageing and sees it as a lifelong process, the more apparent it will become that poverty isn't intrinsic to ageing but results from policies and practices expressing contempt and indifference to older people and to the ageing process itself – and that can be resisted by all of us, whatever our age. (8)

There is much more work to be done to achieve this alternative approach to ageing. The written accounts at the heart of this book suggest some possible ways forward. First, we need to pay more attention to such accounts in themselves rather than seeing them as simply 'primary sources' for selective quotation in support of historical or other forms of academic argument. Second, we need to promote the writing of such accounts as a beneficial and productive act in itself. The kind of writing exemplified by the contributors here gives the lie to any idea of memoirs as simply a passive, retrospective account of the past. Rather, the interplay of past and present suggests how the passing of time is not simply experienced as a linear progression but as a more nuanced interplay of subtly changing values, attitudes and understanding. This revelation is made possible by detailed, written self-reflection, which is itself enabled by cultural and social developments over the lifetimes of the participants included in this volume, such as modernist writing and the evolution of the education system. What this book shows indirectly is that such cultural and social developments were as much an integral element of the welfare state as pensions, hospitals and social care. What it shows directly is the possibility of 'growing old' being a rewarding lifelong process open to everyone, provided supporting social and cultural systems are in place.

Works Cited

Hinton, James. *Seven Lives from Mass Observation*. Oxford: Oxford University Press. 2016.

Hubble, Nick and Philip Tew. *Ageing, Narrative and Identity: New Qualitative Social Research*. Basingstoke: Palgrave Macmillan. 2013.

Karpf, Anne. *How to Age*. Basingstoke: Macmillan. 2014.

May, Theresa. 'Statement from the new Prime Minister Theresa May'. 16 July 2016: https://www.gov.uk/government/speeches/statement-from-the-new-prime-minister-theresa-may.

Segal, Lynne. *Out of Time: The Pleasures and Perils of Ageing*. London: Verso. 2013.

Timmins, Nicholas. *The Five Giants: A Biography of the Welfare State*. Hammersmith: Fontana. 1996.

Appendix: FCMAP, MO
and the U3A

The Fiction and the Cultural Mediation of Ageing Project (FCMAP), which ran from 1 May 2009 until 31 January 2012, was conducted by a research team based in the Brunel Centre for Contemporary Writing (BCCW) at Brunel University, London. The initial FCMAP research questions were concerned with investigating (a) the relationship between cultural representations of, and social attitudes to, ageing and (b) the potential of critical reflection and elective reading by older subjects for engendering new ways of thinking about ageing. In meeting this second objective, it was necessary to develop an approach which limited the influence of the research team on the participants as much as possible in order to foster autonomous thinking processes. Therefore, the FCMAP team had reservations concerning direct interviews with volunteers in the first phase of the project as these would incorporate and represent an unequal set of relationships. Instead, FCMAP set out to assemble an innovative methodological bricolage by refusing to rule out any information in advance and drawing equally on personal narratives, critical reflections on group encounters, responses to fiction and the fictions themselves, with the aim of revealing experiences of, and opinions concerning, ageing that normally remain hidden to public view.

Narrative and fiction seemed particularly germane because of the potential in their synthesis of archetypal, social, quotidian and personal worlds, and their correlation to (if not permeation of) the world of eventfulness and action equally. With these contexts in mind, FCMAP drew on the tradition of the social research organization Mass Observation (MO), which used techniques from poetry and surrealism to compile an 'anthropology of ourselves'. MO was founded in 1937 by Tom Harrisson, Humphrey Jennings and Charles Madge and ran in its first phase until 1949 – for an overview, see Crain (2006). Their projects included a study of the industrial working class in Bolton ('Worktown') and the establishment of a National Panel of volunteers, who answered monthly questionnaires about various aspects of their everyday lives and were, from the outbreak of the war, asked to keep day-to-day personal diaries; the most famous of these was that of Nella Last (1981), memorably portrayed by Victoria Wood in the 2006 TV drama *Housewife 49*. MO was unique in terms of its participative research techniques, capacity to simultaneously reveal and interrogate narratives of everyday life modes of data collection, and pioneering analysis of public opinion (see Hubble 2010).

Diaries of course have the potential to unlock something of the very privately held opinions that other methods of engagement tend not to access and MO's central method might be seen as encouraging members of the public to keep a variety of diaries ranging from the day diaries they collected for the twelfth day of each month during 1937 to the vast diaries kept by observers, including Nella Last and the novelist Naomi Mitchison, during the Second World War. In *Nine Wartime Lives: Mass-Observation and the Making of the Modern Self* (2010), James Hinton notes the unique specificity of these diaries: 'Mass-Observation offered a discipline and a context which transcended the purely private, meeting a need to frame individual quests in relation to larger public purposes' (6). Therefore, he argues that they 'take us as close as a historian can hope to get to observe selfhood under construction' (7). And clearly a sufficient number of such diaries taken together can also offer some view of the manner in which social opinions either emerge or are responded to, as well as providing, through analysis, an informal cartography of aspects of collective group identities. Crucially, Hinton refuses to give ground to those critics who question MO on grounds of how representative it is, by stating explicitly that the biographical examples he discusses open a window on to the personal opinion and everyday life of post-war Britain and are definitely 'not "case studies" narrowly designed to sustain a particular theory or test a particular hypothesis' (20). This was also how the original mass observers understood their project; their analysis involved sifting and accounting for the influence of imposed cultural views upon personal perspectives, thereby allowing them to reveal private opinion at odds with publicly accepted norms as, for example, in their prediction of the 1945 Labour election victory eighteen months in advance (Harrisson 1944). Moreover, in today's 'politically correct' age, when people may be even more wary of candid public utterances, diaries retain this potential to unlock private views and reveal their interaction with wider social and cultural narratives.

Since 1981, a contemporary MO Project (MOP) has been run from the MO Archive (MOA) at the University of Sussex. This is one of the longest-running longitudinal life-writing projects anywhere in the world. Three times a year, MO participants receive a seasonal 'directive', which is a set of open questions that invite them to write freely and discursively about their views and experiences. Anne Jamieson and Christina Victor's edited collection, *Researching Ageing and Later Life: The Practice of Social Gerontology* (2002), includes an article on the MOP by Dorothy Sheridan, which enumerates the particular attributes that make it particularly suitable for ageing research. First, the majority of respondents are not only over fifty but also well distributed across the older age ranges. Second, the longitudinal nature of the MOP means that, for example, at the turn of the millennium they had eighteen respondents in the over-eighty age range who had been writing for over fifteen years, providing a vast wealth of material. The same holds true across all the age ranges, as Sheridan observes:

> The project itself is a record of the ageing process over 20 years, whether someone goes from 32 to 52, or from 62 to 82, and if again is taken to means the process of growing older at any point in one's life, then we have access here to a huge amount of information about the life span (75).

Third, the particular quality of MO, as opposed to other forms of life writing such as memoirs and autobiographies, is that it does not provide one single monolithic account of a life. Rather, reading across the directive replies of an individual over the years reveals layered life stories made up of description and re-description, which 'enable us to have access to the contradictions of everyday life, and to the changes of people's perceptions of themselves and the world they inhabit' (75). MO material has been used successfully in ageing research ranging from Pat Thane's *Old Age in English History: Past Experiences, Present Issues* (2000) to Bill Bytheway's work on ageing and birthdays (2005, 2009, 2011).

For these two reasons, that is its capacity to reveal private opinion and its pedigree in ageing research, FCMAP made MO diary-keeping techniques central to the two major studies it set up, following Chris Phillipson's (2007: vii) proposals for a critical gerontology, both to give voice directly to older subjects and to include them centrally in the research process: one involving the present-day MO and the other ninety volunteers from the older age ranges organized into reading and discussion groups. For the first of these, an MO directive was commissioned by the FCMAP team, and issued in winter 2009, concerning participants' responses to representations of ageing in political and media discourse (although in the interests of not influencing response, this part of the directive was titled 'Books and You' and only the final question directly investigated 'how your age group is represented'). The directive was sent to the panel of around 600 people, and 193 written responses were returned. In conjunction with earlier directives concerning ageing in winter 1992, whose responses are featured in Thane (2000), and autumn 2006, it was possible to collate high-quality longitudinal qualitative data regarding how ageing is understood in society, how this differs between generations and how social expectations regarding ageing relate to self-understanding. Findings from this MO part of the study are discussed in chapters three, four and five of Nick Hubble and Philip Tew's *Ageing, Narrative and Identity* (2013) and the three directives are reproduced in the appendix to that volume.

For the other parallel strand of research conducted by FCMAP, eight volunteer reading groups (VRGs) were set up in collaboration with the Third Age Trust, involving eighty volunteers who were in an age range from their early sixties to their nineties. The volunteers were arranged into reading groups located in the following district associations of the University of the Third Age (U3A): Banstead (which was given the code CBL), Camden Town (OUL), Highgate/North London 1 (NOL), Highgate/North London 2 (HIL), Kingston (KSL), South East London (SEL), Tower Hamlets (THL) and Waterloo (WMC). Over the period of a year (2009–2010), all groups read nine nominated novels published from 1944 to the present, a period that corresponded largely with the adult life experiences of participants, and met once a month to discuss each book and the various ageing-related issues arising. The novels were (in order of reading) David Lodge's *Deaf Sentence* (2008), Jim Crace's *Arcadia* (1992), Caryl Phillips's *A Distant Shore* (2003), Hanif Kureishi's *The Body* (2002), Trezza Azzopardi's *Remember Me* (2004), Angela Carter's *Wise Children* (1991), Barbara Pym's *Quartet in Autumn* (1977), Norah Hoult's *There Were No Windows* (1944) and Fay Weldon's *Chalcot Crescent* (2009). Groups were allowed to substitute one book from this list with another from a 'B' list: Muriel Spark's *Memento Mori* (1959), Angus Wilson's *Late Call* (1964), Elizabeth Taylor's *Mrs Palfrey at the Claremount* (1971), Margaret Forster's *The Seduction of Mrs Pendlebury* (1974), Jonathan Coe's *What a Carve Up?* (1994), Mark Haddon's *A Spot of Bother* (2006) and Anita Brookner's *Strangers* (2009). These novels, many of which are described and discussed in chapter five of *Ageing, Narrative and Identity*, were chosen to provide a range of contrasting vantage points on later life and also for the thought-provoking ways in which their presentation might engage and mobilize the readers' attitudes and assumptions. Reading group members – using a personally allocated code relating to the reading group in which they participated to ensure anonymity – kept diaries recording their responses to each book during *and* after reading it and again after the group discussion of the book. In doing the latter, most respondents opted generally to reflect upon the other readers' views and the themes arising from such discussions. Many of these diaries are digitally archived on the UK Data Service website (http://reshare.ukdataservice.ac.uk/850580/).

A number of authors of the books on the reading list discussed their novels and the topic of ageing, as well as answering questions, in a series of (recorded) interviews and public events organized by the project team, to which the reading-group members were invited. An audience of over 220 came to Brunel on 3 February 2010 to see Jim Crace and David Lodge in discussion; about 150 came to hear Caryl Phillips in Central London on 19 March 2010; over 70 attended the Trezza Azzopardi daytime talk at Brunel on 10 June 2010; and finally about 250 listened to Fay Weldon discuss ageing with Will Self at Brunel on 8 April 2011 (see Self 2011).

From the beginning of the project, in order to make the insights revealed directly available to policymakers, the FCMAP team collaborated with researchers from the think tank Demos (who had offered advice on developing the structure of the project before its commencement) and supplied them with regular analytical reports on the material coming in from both the U3A reading groups and the longitudinal study of the MO data. This process culminated in the intense collaborative drafting of a 200-page report *Coming of Age*, published as a paperback in April 2011 and simultaneously made available online in PDF format. *Coming of Age* was launched at the FCMAP 'New Cultures of Ageing Conference', held at Brunel University on the 8th–9th April 2011, during which panels of speakers including Professor Pat Thane, Professor Dorothy Sheridan (MO), Keith Richards (U3A), Louise Bazalgette (Demos) and members of the FCMAP team presented and discussed topics such as third- and fourth-age subjectivity and ageing policy. The day culminated with the aforementioned public debate between Will Self and Fay Weldon. Subsequently, the FCMAP team and Demos researchers presented the report findings to national, regional, local government and third sector stakeholders at the 'Coming of Age Policy Roundtable' hosted by Demos at their headquarters in Tooley Street, London, on 16 May. Academic publications from the project include *Ageing, Narrative and Identity* and Nick Hubble and Philip Tew's journal article, '"There Is No Doubt that I'm Old": Everyday Narratives of Ageing' (2014).

This book directly results from the Economic and Social Research Council (ESRC)–funded follow-on project to FCMAP, 'New Narratives of Everyday Ageing in Contemporary Britain', which ran at Brunel from 1 September 2012 to 31 August 2013, with the aim of producing this anthology of new narratives of ageing.

Works Cited and Further Reading

Bazalgette, Louise, John Holden, Philip Tew, Nick Hubble, and Jago Morrison. *Coming of Age*. London: Demos (2011): https://www.demos.co.uk/files/Coming_of_Age_-_web.pdf?1302099024.

Bytheway, Bill. 'Age-identities and the Celebration of Birthdays'. *Ageing & Society*, 25, 2005: 463–477.

Bytheway, Bill. 'Writing about Age, Birthdays and the Passage of Time'. *Ageing & Society*, 29, 2009: 883–901.

Bytheway, Bill. *Unmasking Age: The Significance of Age for Social Research.* Bristol: Policy Press. 2011.

Crain, Caleb. 'Surveillance Society: The Mass Observation Movement and the Meaning of Everyday Life'. *New Yorker* (11 September 2006): www.newyorker.com/archive/2006/09/11/060911crat_atlarge.

Harrisson, Tom. 'Who'll Win?' *Political Quarterly*, XV (1), 1944: 21–32.

Hinton, James. *Nine Wartime Diaries: Mass-Observation and the Making of the Modern Self.* Oxford: Oxford University Press. 2010.

Hubble, Nick. *Mass Observation and Everyday Life: Culture, History, Theory.* Rev. 2nd ed. Basingstoke: Palgrave Macmillan. 2010.

Hubble, Nick and Philip Tew. *Ageing, Narrative and Identity: New Qualitative Social Research.* Basingstoke: Palgrave Macmillan. 2013.

Hubble, Nick and Philip Tew. '"There Is No Doubt that I'm Old": Everyday Narratives of Ageing' in 'Ageing and Fiction', special issue, *EnterText*, 11, Winter, 2014. 139–157: http://www.brunel.ac.uk/__data/assets/pdf_file/0003/397803/8-entertext-ageing-hubble-tew-there-is-no-doubt-that-i-am-old-everyday-narratives-of-ageing.pdf.

Jamieson, Anne and Christina R. Victor (eds.). *Researching Ageing and Later Life: The Practice of Social Gerontology.* Milton Keynes: Open University Press. 2002.

Last, Nella. *Nella Last's War: A Mother's Diary 1939–45.* Eds. Richard Broad and Suzie Fleming. Bristol: Falling Wall Press. 1981.

Phillipson, Chris. 'Foreword'. In Miriam Bernard and Thomas Scharf (eds.). *Critical Perspectives on Ageing Societies.* Bristol: Policy Press, 2007: vii–viii.

Self, Will. 'The Older People Get, The Older They Believe "Old" to Be: Review of Lewis Wolpert, *You're Looking Very Well'*. *Guardian* (30 April 2011): http://www.guardian.co.uk/books/2011/may/01/looking-very-well-lewis-wolpert-review.

Sheridan, Dorothy. 'Using the Mass-observation Archive'. In Anne Jamieson and Christina R. Victor (eds.). *Researching Ageing and Later Life: The Practice of Social Gerontology.* Milton Keynes: Open University Press, 2002: 66–79.

Thane, Pat. *Old Age in English History: Past Experiences, Present Issues.* Oxford: Oxford University Press. 2000.

Bibliography

Bazalgette, Louise, John Holden, Philip Tew, Nick Hubble and Jago Morrison. *Coming of Age*. London: Demos. 2011: https://www.demos.co.uk/files/Coming_of_Age_-_web.pdf?1302099024.

Bytheway, Bill. 'Age-identities and the Celebration of Birthdays'. *Ageing & Society*, 25, 2005: 463–477.

Bytheway, Bill. 'Writing about Age, Birthdays and the Passage of Time'. *Ageing & Society*, 29, 2009: 883–901.

Bytheway, Bill. *Unmasking Age: The Significance of Age for Social Research*. Bristol: Policy Press. 2011.

Crain, Caleb. 'Surveillance Society: The Mass Observation Movement and the Meaning of Everyday Life'. *New Yorker* (11 September 2006): www.newyorker.com/archive/2006/09/11/060911crat_atlarge.

Harrisson, Tom. 'Who'll Win?' *Political Quarterly*, XV (1), 1944: 21–32.

Hinton, James. *Nine Wartime Diaries: Mass-observation and the Making of the Modern Self*. Oxford: Oxford University Press. 2010.

Hinton, James. *Seven Lives from Mass Observation*. Oxford: Oxford University Press. 2016.

Hubble, Nick. *Mass Observation and Everyday Life: Culture, History, Theory*. Rev. 2nd ed. Basingstoke: Palgrave Macmillan. 2010.

Hubble, Nick and Philip Tew. *Ageing, Narrative and Identity: New Qualitative Social Research*. Basingstoke: Palgrave Macmillan. 2013.

Hubble, Nick and Philip Tew. '"There Is No Doubt that I'm Old": Everyday Narratives of Ageing' in 'Ageing and Fiction', special issue, *EnterText*, 11, Winter, 2014. 139–157: http://www.brunel.ac.uk/__data/assets/pdf_file/0003/397803/8-entertext-ageing-hubble-tew-there-is-no-doubt-that-i-am-old-everyday-narratives-of-ageing.pdf.

Jamieson, Anne and Christina R. Victor (eds.). *Researching Ageing and Later Life: The Practice of Social Gerontology*. Milton Keynes: Open University Press, 2002.

Karpf, Anne. *How to Age*. Basingstoke: Macmillan. 2014.

Langhamer, Claire. *The English in Love: The Intimate Story of an Emotional Revolution*. Oxford: Oxford University Press. 2013.

Laslett, Peter. *A Fresh Map of Life*. Basingstoke: Macmillan. 1996 [1989].

Last, Nella. *Nella Last's War: A Mother's Diary 1939–45*. Eds. Richard Broad and Suzie Fleming. Bristol: Falling Wall Press. 1981.

May, Theresa. 'Statement from the new Prime Minister Theresa May' (16 July 2016): https://www.gov.uk/government/speeches/statement-from-the-new-prime-minister-theresa-may.

Phillipson, Chris. 'Foreword'. In Miriam Bernard and Thomas Scharf (eds.). *Critical Perspectives on Ageing Societies*. Bristol: Policy Press, 2007: vii–viii.

Segal, Lynne. *Out of Time: The Pleasures and Perils of Ageing.* London: Verso. 2013.

Self, Will. 'The Older People Get, The Older They Believe "Old" to Be: Review of Lewis Wolpert, *You're Looking Very Well'*. *Guardian* (30 April 2011): http://www.guardian.co.uk/books/2011/may/01/looking-very-well-lewis-wolpert-review.

Sheridan, Dorothy (2002). 'Using the Mass-observation Archive'. In Anne Jamieson and Christina R. Victor (eds.). *Researching Ageing and Later Life: The Practice of Social Gerontology.* Milton Keynes: Open University Press, 2002: 66–79.

Thane, Pat. *Old Age in English History: Past Experiences, Present Issues.* Oxford: Oxford University Press. 2000.

Timmins, Nicholas. *The Five Giants: A Biography of the Welfare State.* Hammersmith: Fontana. 1996.

Index